CONTENTS

1
INTRODUCTION

Frontiers

'Space', says the voice at the beginning of the space fiction series *Star Trek*, 'Space – the final frontier'. This is true in the imaginary world of inter-planetary adventure. It is also true in our world today. We have explored the continents of this planet. We have mapped coastlines and plotted rivers. We have measured mountains and deserts. Most of the fertile land is being farmed. Oil, coal and other minerals are drilled and dug from beneath the surface of the earth. Villages, towns and cities have been built wherever we have settled. Even the great white wastes of Antarctica have been surveyed and are known to teams of scientists. If we want to travel to uncharted lands and explore unknown continents we must now cross the frontier of space to other planets and other solar systems.

It was not, of course, always like this. Only in the twentieth century has the whole earth been charted and known. Before this there were frontiers on earth – land frontiers. These frontiers divided the known and settled lands from the unknown and unsettled. Sometimes the frontier would be obvious – a range of mountains, a river or a desert. Sometimes it would be a line drawn on a map by a government, a queen or an emperor. Some frontiers were permanent, agreed between the owners or rulers of the land. Others were not, and were pushed further and further out as men and women explored and settled land which previously had been unknown.

The story of America and the American West is the story of a frontier being pushed west by the dogged determination of ordinary men and women. It is an exciting story of courage and bravery, despair and failure, hard work and prosperity, and treachery and greed.

The natural frontiers of North America

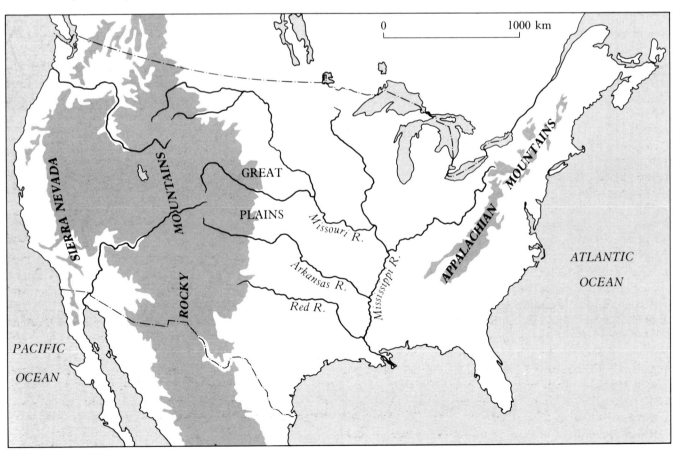

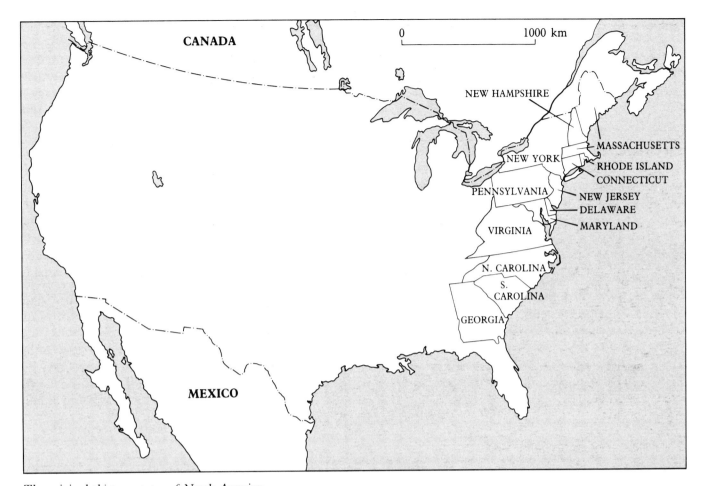

The original thirteen states of North America

The natural frontiers of America

You can see from the map opposite that America has natural frontiers which, in the eighteenth and nineteenth centuries, made it difficult for people to push westwards across the continent. This meant that ordinary men and women would only try to cross these natural barriers when they became desperate. They would only struggle over mountains, rivers and plains when their need to leave the places which they knew was greater than their fear of the unknown.

The Appalachian mountains, rising to heights of 2000 metres, with steep rock faces and deep valleys, kept the first white settlers on the eastern coast of the continent. The Mississippi River, wide, slow and treacherous, formed the next natural frontier. Beyond the Mississippi came the prairie grasslands and Great Plains. Dry, arid, with sudden storms, scorching sun and droughts, the Plains were quite a different frontier. They stretched for hundreds of kilometres to the foothills of the Rockies and the Sierra Nevada. These mountain chains were themselves over 1000 kilometres wide and reached heights of over 5 kilometres, with deep ravines and high mountain passes which were completely blocked by snow for months every winter. They were the final natural frontier, standing in the way of people moving westwards.

Lines on the map

The natural frontiers of America, however, are only part of the story. We must look also at the frontiers which people have drawn.

In 1783 the thirteen states on the map above were all that there was of the United States of America. Ten years earlier these states had been colonies belonging to Great Britain. Between 1776 and 1783 the thirteen colonies fought Britain and British rule and finally gained their independence. They became the first American states. There was, however, a great deal more to the continent of America than these thirteen states. In the 1780s parts of the rest of the continent were still unknown to Europeans. Parts had been claimed and occupied by the British, the Spanish and the French. Yet by 1848 the United States government was to own all of present day America from the Atlantic to the Pacific coasts, and from the Canadian to the Mexican borders. How had this come about?

Pushing westwards

By 1800 American settlers had pushed the frontier with the West as far as the Mississippi River. Here the expansion of America westwards stopped. Not only was the Mississippi a natural frontier itself, but Spain owned vast lands west of the river. The United States watched helplessly while Spain sold part of the Mississippi valley to France, as well as her claim to the prairies and plains west of the river. France, however, needed money for a war in Europe. In 1803 the French government quickly sold all this land, the Louisiana Purchase, as it was called, to the United States for $15 million. The USA now owned the whole of the centre of America. The way westward was open once more.

In 1804 the President of the USA sent two American explorers, Meriwether Lewis and William Clark, to explore the Louisiana Purchase. Meriwether Lewis and William Clark managed to cross over the Rockies and Sierra Nevada to the Pacific coast. They claimed for the USA all the lands through which they travelled beyond Lousiana. Lewis and Clark's expedition was the first journey overland from the Mississippi westwards to the sea. They had proved

that such a journey was possible; they had charted the headwaters of the Missouri and Columbia Rivers, and they had learned how high and wide the Rockies and Sierra Nevada really were. Their journals inspired others to push the frontier westwards.

It was not enough, however, just to reach the Pacific coast and to claim land for the United States government. Great Britain owned Oregon, and Mexico owned California. As early as 1818, as you can see on the map, Great Britain had tidied up the frontier between Canada and the United States. In 1846 Britain and the USA finally agreed that the border between British Canada and the United States should be the 49th parallel. Canada would keep Vancouver Island and the United States would own all of Oregon south of the border with Canada.

There was still the problem of California, however. California, like Texas, was owned by Mexico. The Mexican government had encouraged Americans to settle in both California and Texas. When American settlers began to outnumber Mexicans in California and Texas they demanded a larger and larger say in the way both countries were run. War between the United States and Mexico had been threatening for some years over this and other matters. It finally

The growth of North America 1783–1853

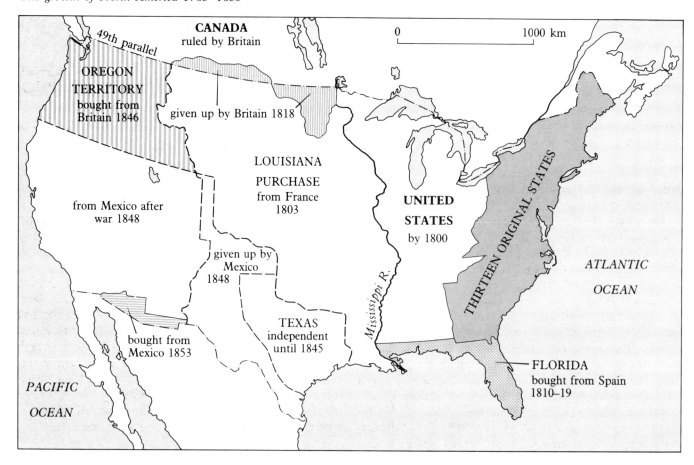

A contemporary etching of the Lewis and Clark expedition of 1804

broke out in 1846. Mexico didn't stand a chance. American troops poured over the frontier and invaded from the sea. Mexico was forced to surrender. The United States gained all Mexican lands north of the Rio Grande and Gildas Rivers. This included California.

Meanwhile, what had been happening in Texas? There, Americans like Davy Crockett and Sam Houston had taken part in a revolution and in 1836 Texas was declared independent of Mexico. It was not until 1844, however, that Texas became an American state.

By 1853, through a combination of luck, force, treaties and money, the United States owned the whole of the land of America from coast to coast and from Canada to Mexico. No one knew, however, whether they would be able to hold on to this land. Would Mexico become strong enough to challenge the American hold on Texas and California? Would France regret the sale of Louisiana? Would Britain try to alter the Canadian border and grow worried about the position of Vancouver? As far as the United States government was concerned, the only way to hold on to the land was to fill it with loyal Americans.

This, then, is the story of the American West. It is the story of the way in which ordinary men and women pushed the frontier of settlement further and further west beyond the Mississippi River. In doing this they fulfilled their own personal ambitions, and the dream that Americans would live and work on all the land between the east and west coasts.

The lands beyond the Mississippi, though, were not empty lands. The people who lived there were a people with different hopes, different ambitions and different beliefs from those of the white Americans. They were the native peoples of America – the north American Indians. The story of the American West, then, is not only about pushing the frontier of settlement westwards. It is also about the dramatic and bitter clash between these two groups – the white people and the Indians.

2

THE PLAINS INDIANS

When you hear the words 'North American Indians', how do you picture them? A proud chief, standing tall in his long feathered head-dress? A brave warrior on a bareback horse, galloping for his life and shooting arrows at buffalo and white men? A black-haired squaw with a baby strapped to her back? All of these ideas would be right, but they only describe part of the story. Who were the Indians? How did they come to be living in America? Why did they develop a way of life which was so different from that of white people?

America's Indians

Twenty thousand years ago America was not a separate continent as it is today. It was linked to Asia by a great land mass which joined present-day Alaska to present-day Siberia. Across this enormous land bridge wandered great herds of European and Asian animals.

Why did people follow the animals into America? Geologists and archaeologists, digging through the frozen rocks of Alaska and the hot sandy deserts of Arizona, have discovered ancient stone fireplaces and arrow heads which were made by people living in these places many thousands of years ago. Discoveries like these have helped archaeologists and historians to decide that men and women followed the animals because they were hunting them. The beasts which they followed were big animals which gave a lot of meat. The animals moved in large herds, which made it easy for people to follow them and kill them for the food which they provided. The hunters moved down through America, following the trails left by the animals. These trails led them to sheltered valleys, water, and, in the end, to the very heart of America – the Great Plains.

The gentle movement of people and animals from Europe and Asia into America, however, was to stop. About nine thousand years ago the sea came crashing and roaring across the great land bridge, and America was cut off from Asia for ever. By this time the people whom the Europeans later called 'Indians' were firmly established in America. Indeed, there were many different tribes and nations of Indians, living in the rocky mountains, the dry plains, the wooded valleys and the sandy desert fringes. They had all learned how to adapt their lives to the

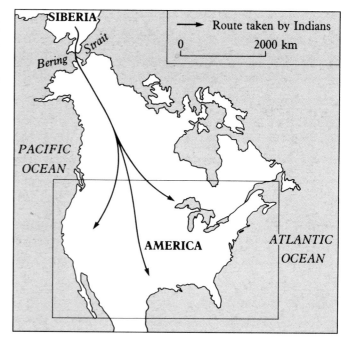

How the Indians came to North America

surroundings in which they lived. The Iroquois in the fertile east, for example, were farmers and fishermen; the Teton Sioux on the Plains were hunters, and the Bannock and Ute tribes in the mountain regions lived on berries, roots and grubs.

Why the Plains Indians?

The Indians we will be concentrating on in this book are the Plains Indians – mainly the Cheyenne, Arapaho, Comanche, Kiowa and Kiowa Apache on the southern Plains, and the Crows and Sioux to the north. This is because they played a very important part in the history of the American West. It was the Plains Indians who fiercely resisted the white people in their attempt to push the frontier westward across the Great Plains to the Pacific coast. It was the Plains Indians who had their way of life altered for ever by successive waves of white people – cattle men and cowboys, pioneers and homesteaders – all of whom wanted to use the Great Plains for their own purposes. It was the Plains Indians who stood in the way of white Americans who believed that America was there to make the white people rich and prosperous.

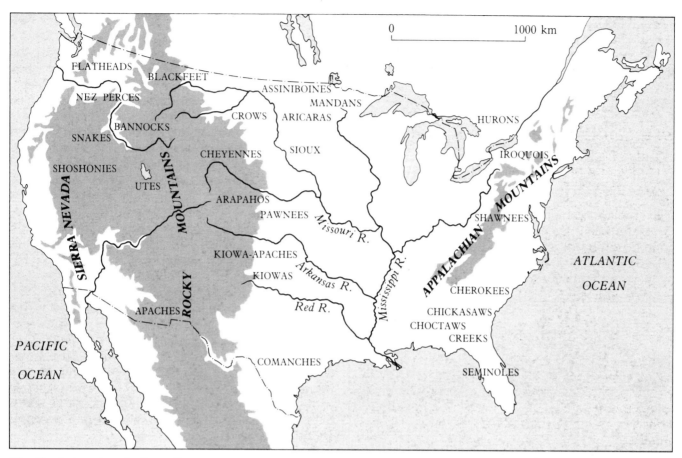

The North American Indian tribes

Horses and hunters

For a long time the Plains Indians were poor tribes, living difficult and dangerous lives, often close to starvation. The Plains themselves were bare and empty, except for the huge herds of buffalo which drifted over the vast empty spaces, grazing wherever the grass was sweetest. The Indians lived on the fringes of the Great Plains, along the banks of trickling muddy rivers. They grew maize and beans, and sometimes hunted buffalo when they needed meat. They used to cover themselves with animal skins to disguise their human smell, and crawl on all fours to try to kill the buffalo.

What happened to turn these people, struggling to survive on the Great Plains, into proud chiefs and brave warriors, ready and able to challenge the white Americans who came with their advanced technology, their dreams and their greed? The answer lies quite simply in one animal: the horse.

There were no horses in America when the Indians arrived there. Horses did not cross the vast land bridge between Asia and America with humans and the other animals. How, then, did the Indians come to own horses?

Horses were taken to America by Europeans just over 400 years ago. In 1540 men from Spain, sailing westwards in search of treasure and adventure, landed in Central America. They brought with them horses and guns. These were two things which the Indians had never seen before. The Spaniards conquered the Indian tribes living in Central America. They built towns and began to breed horses. However, they would not sell horses to the Indians under any circumstances. In 1640 the Pueblo Indians rose up against the Spaniards. They drove them out and captured their horses. The Pueblo, however, were not great hunters and so did not really need the horses. They kept some for meat and some for breeding, and sold the rest to other Indian tribes.

So the Plains Indians came to own horses, and their lives were never the same again. The horse meant power. The horse meant freedom. Without horses, these tribes might have stayed for ever scratching a living along river banks and occasionally hunting buffalo on foot. With horses, they could follow the huge herds of buffalo over the Great Plains and hunt them much more efficiently. The Indians' way of life had changed for ever. For ever, that is, until the white people came to the Plains.

The Plains Indians became marvellous horse riders, skilled at hunting, fighting and sport. George Catlin, an American artist who travelled amongst them for eight years in the 1830s, wrote:

'. . . the Comanches are the most extraordinary horsemen that I have ever seen in all my travels. . . . A Comanche on his feet is out of his element, awkward as a monkey on the ground . . . but the moment he lays his hands upon his horse his face even becomes handsome, and he gracefully flies away like a different being.'

The Indians certainly prized their horses. They thought of them as important warriors, as you can see from these drawings of Sioux war ponies. The ponies are painted with designs which were just as special as those with which the Indians painted themselves.

The Sioux Indians decorated their ponies like this for war

The beliefs of the Plains Indians

The Great Spirit

All Indians believed in the Great Spirit, called Waken Tanka by the Sioux. The Great Spirit ruled over everything. He lived in the Happy Hunting Ground, a beautiful country beyond the skies. The Indians' greatest hope was to go to the Happy Hunting Ground when they died, and they were only likely to do this if they had served the Great Spirit well during their lifetime.

As well as believing in the one Great Spirit, the Plains Indians believed that all natural things had spirits of their own. This meant that humans, animals, insects, fish, plants and birds all had to be treated with the same sort of respect. There was a closeness between man and all natural things because Indians believed that *all* life was holy. Man was no more important than any other living creature.

There was, however, more to the Indians' religious beliefs than simply a feeling of oneness with nature. This feeling and love grew from an understanding of the powerful forces which were at work within nature. Plains Indians were convinced that the power of the earth always moved and worked in circles. Circles came to have tremendous importance and significance. Circles were all around them. The sky was round and so was the sun which shone in it; the wind whirled in circles, and the seasons formed one great circle, always coming back to where they started. Therefore, the Indians reasoned, the power of the earth surrounded them. Even the life of man was a circle, beginning with childhood and ending up with very old people behaving like children. Birds built their nests in circles, and the Indians themselves set their homes, their tepees, in circles.

The Indians knew that they could only use this power of the earth if they understood the natural world properly, and tried to work with it and not against it. Indians would never try to disrupt the natural order of things. Their one aim was to understand the forces which surrounded them. Indians could then work with these forces and their power would become the Indians' power.

An Arapaho Indian pouch with a sacred circle design

A modern photograph of the 'medicine wheel' on Medicine Mountain in Wyoming, a circle deliberately built by the Indians

SOURCE WORK: The Great Spirit

SOURCE A

'Our land here is the dearest thing on earth to us.'

(White Thunder – a Sioux Indian, in Dee Brown, *Bury My Heart at Wounded Knee*, Barrie and Jenkins 1971)

SOURCE B

'I never want to leave my country; all my relatives are lying in the ground, and when I fall to pieces, I am going to fall to pieces here.'

(Wolf Necklace – a Sioux Indian, in Dee Brown, *Bury My Heart at Wounded Knee*)

SOURCE C

'My friend, I am going to tell you the story of my life. It is the story of all that is holy and good to tell, and of us two leggeds sharing it with the four leggeds and the wings of the air – all green things; for these are children of one mother and their father is one spirit.'

(Black Elk – Holy Man of the Oglala Sioux, in J. Neihardt, *Black Elk Speaks*, Sphere Books 1974)

SOURCE D

'The Sioux was a true lover of nature. He loved the earth and all things of the earth . . . their tepees were built upon the earth. The birds that flew in the air came to rest upon the earth, and it was the final abiding place of all things that lived and grew. Kinship with all creatures of the earth, sky and water was a real and active belief.'

(Sioux Chief Luther Standing Bear, *Land of the Spotted Eagle*, Houghton Mifflin 1933)

1 Explain carefully whether or not you agree with these statements about the Plains Indians' beliefs:
a) Only man was holy among the animals.
b) The strongest power in the world was the Great Spirit.

c) Circles were important only because birds made round nests.
d) Indians had to defeat the Great Spirit in order to become powerful themselves.

2 Read Sources A, B, C and D. What do they tell you about:
a) Indians' feelings about the land?
b) Indians' feelings about living things?

SOURCE E

These are names which Black Elk said were given to the months.

January	Moon of the Frost in the Tepee
February	Moon of the Dark Red Calves
March	Moon of the Snow Blind
April	Moon of the Red Grass Appearing
May	Moon when the Ponies Shed
June	Moon of Making Fat
July	Moon of the Red Cherries
August	Moon when the Cherries turn Black
September	Moon when the Calves grow Hair
October	Moon of the Changing Season
November	Moon of the Falling Leaves
December	Moon of the Popping Trees

(Black Elk, in J. Neihardt, *Black Elk Speaks*)

3 Read Source E.
a) Why do you think the Sioux Indians gave the months these names?
b) How was it possible that the whole Sioux nation understood what time of year was meant by these names?
c) Other Indian tribes and nations had different names for the months of the year. What can be found out about a tribe from the names which it gives to the months?

4 Explain carefully how *all* the sources in this section help you to understand what Chief Joseph of the Nez Perce Indians meant when he said: 'The Earth and myself are of one mind'.

Visions

Visions were very important to all Indians. They believed that it was through visions that they could come into contact with the spirits and with the one Great Spirit which flows through the universe.

On page 13 you can read of one Indian's vision. This Indian was Black Elk, who became a holy man of the Oglala Sioux tribe. When he was very young he had a powerful vision, but told no one at all about it until he was much older. Perhaps he was afraid to tell because he thought he would not be believed. Perhaps he was afraid to tell because it was too private and personal to be shared. Perhaps he was afraid it would be wrongly interpreted. Whatever the reason, it is clear that Black Elk's vision was very important to him.

Black Elk was not alone. All Indians wanted to have one vision which was special to them. Indian boys had to go looking for their vision. They went to a sweat lodge where they prepared their bodies by making sure they were clean, and prepared their minds by fasting (going without food) and praying. Once he had received his vision, the young man

Part of a painting on an animal skin showing an Apache girl's puberty ceremony

would return to his tribe. The Medicine Man would interpret the vision; everyone would rejoice, and the young man would receive his adult name. This adult name had to be connected with his vision. When he was a child, an Indian boy might be called 'No Teeth' or 'Fat Toes'. After his vision he would become 'Sitting Bull' or 'Grey Raven' or 'Running Water', depending upon what was in his vision. No one thought it shameful if an Indian boy did not receive a vision the first time he prepared himself for one. This simply meant that he was not yet ready.

It was different for girls. Indians believed that girls could easily and readily make contact with the spirit world. When a girl began her monthly periods she automatically had the power to talk freely with the spirits. The only problem for the girl and for her tribe was in learning how to control these spirits before they controlled her. She was taken away by an old medicine woman and when she had learned how to control the spirits properly she was returned to her tribe and to her family. She was immediately given her adult name, amid much ceremony, rejoicing and feasting.

Medicine men

The medicine man was important because it was he who interpreted the visions of young people. But this was not the only work he had to do for the tribe. The medicine man was vital to the tribe because he could make contact with the spirits of all living things. Everything he did, from interpreting visions to curing the sick, stemmed from this. The Indians believed that a medicine man could cure sickness *because* he could use the power of the spirits; he could interpret visions *because* of his closeness to the spirit world. The medicine man should really be called the 'mystery man', because he was the tribe's most important link with the spirit world.

Each male Indian had his own medicine or 'mystery'. This was kept in a small bag which he wore around his neck always. The little bag contained sacred objects – a bird's claw, a flower, perhaps – which had sacred and special importance to that particular Indian. He told no one what was in his bag, and when he died it was buried with him. Girls and squaws did not need a medicine bag. They had all the power they needed because they could so easily make contact with the spirit world.

The medicine man was important to individual Indians and to the whole tribe. He was consulted by the chiefs and the Council before war was declared, before peace was made, before the tribe moved hunting grounds, before, in fact, they decided anything important.

SOURCE WORK: Visions and medicine men

SOURCE A

'It was when I was five years old that my grandfather made me a bow and some arrows. The grass was young and I was on horseback. A thunderstorm was coming from where the sun goes down, and just as I was riding into the woods along a creek there was a kingbird sitting on a branch. This was not a dream. It happened. I was going to shoot the kingbird with the bow my grandfather made, when the bird spoke and said:

"The clouds all over are one sided."

Perhaps it meant that all the clouds were looking at me. And then it said:

"Listen! A voice is calling you!"

Then I looked up at the clouds and two men were coming there, headfirst like arrows slanting down. As they came they sang a sacred song and the thunder was like drumming. I will sing it for you. The song and the drumming went like this:

"Behold a sacred voice is calling you;
All over the sky a sacred voice is calling."

I sat there gazing at them and they were coming from the place where the giant lives. But when they were very close to me they wheeled about towards where the sun goes down, and suddenly they were geese. Then they were gone, and the rain came with a big sound and a roaring.'

(Black Elk, in J. Neihardt, *Black Elk Speaks*)

1 Read Source A.
   a) How does this source help us to understand the Indians' closeness to nature?
   b) Why were visions like this important to Indian boys?
   c) Does the fact that Indian boys had visions, and Indian girls did not, make the girls inferior to the boys?

SOURCE B

A drawing by George Catlin of a Blackfoot medicine man in the 1830s. He is covered by the skin of a yellow bear and has snakes and other animals dangling over him

2 Look at Source B.
   a) Which of the following reasons *best* explains why the medicine man looked like this?
      i) He wanted to frighten his own tribe into believing what he said.
      ii) He wanted to frighten white men away from his tribe.
      iii) He was wearing sacred objects to bring himself closer to the Great Spirit.
      iv) He was wearing sacred objects in order to keep the power of the Great Spirit away from the tribe.
   b) Perhaps he didn't look like this at all, and Catlin simply drew him looking fearsome to make his book more interesting!
      i) How could you check whether or not medicine men looked like this?
      ii) How could you check the reasons why medicine men looked as they did?
   c) Why was the medicine man such an important member of every tribe?

SOURCE WORK: Medicine

SOURCE A

'Young men go up on to a hill, and cry and pray for some animal or bird to come to them. For five or six days they neither eat nor drink, and they become thin. While in this state they dream, and whatever animal or bird they see in their dreams becomes their medicine and guardian through life. They are also told in a dream what description of herbs or roots to gather as their medicine, and this they collect and put carefully into a small bag as a charm. They also kill the animal they dreamed of and keep its skin as a charm. No one knows what is the medicine they have gathered; it is kept as a secret. The little bag is kept in the tent, and no one may touch it but the owner.'

(J. G. Frazer, *The Native Races of America*, Lund Humphries 1939)

SOURCE B

'An infant's navel cord was cut immediately after birth and put into a small decorated bag that was retained for life, often worn around the neck. This was the individual's personal medicine. Just as the navel cord provided the link between the baby in the womb and the woman who gave it life, so the medicine acted as a link between the person and the spiritual world. The medicine was not just a symbol, but its loss or destruction meant spiritual death. . . . The actual contents of the bundle were known only to the holder. As the owner matured and his spiritual strength became greater, the contents of the bundle were added to. The bundle was buried with the owner when he died.'

(M. Campbell, *People of the Buffalo*, Douglas and McIntyre 1976)

1 Read Sources A and B, both of which are about medicine bags.
  a) Below is a list of statements about medicine bags. Copy the list into your file, and beside each statement write the letter(s) of the source (either A or B or both) to which it refers.
    i) Indians owned medicine bags from the moment they were born.
    ii) An Indian boy's navel cord was put into his medicine bag.
    iii) Objects could only be put into a medicine bag after an Indian boy had had his vision.
    iv) Only the owner knew what was in his medicine bag.
    v) Only the owner could touch his medicine bag.
  b) Does this difference between the sources mean that one of them must be wrong?

SOURCE C

This extract is from the story of Geronimo, a great Apache medicine man.

'The Indians knew what herbs to use for medicine, how to prepare them and how to give the medicine. This they had been taught in the beginning, and each generation had men who were skilled in the art of healing, in gathering herbs, in preparing them, and in administering the medicine. As much faith was held in prayer as in the actual effect of the medicine.'

(S. M. Barrett (ed.), *Geronimo: His Own Story*, Sphere Books 1974)

SOURCE D

'Medicine is a great word in this country. It is very necessary that one should know the meaning of it. The word medicine means mystery and nothing else.'

(G. Catlin, *Manners, Customs and Conditions of North American Indians*, Vol. 2, Chatto and Windus 1844)

2 Read Sources C and D.
  a) Do Geronimo and George Catlin mean different things by 'medicine'?
  b) Do the sources in this section support George Catlin's meaning of the word?
  c) Geronimo, who wrote Source C, was an Apache medicine man. George Catlin, who wrote Source D, was a white man who had lived among the Indians. Does this mean that George Catlin must have been wrong about medicine?

Dances

Medicine men could always make contact with the spirits, and, at times, so could individual Indians. When there was great trouble, however, the tribe as a whole needed to make contact with the spirits. They did this through many ceremonies and rituals. In all of these the medicine man took a leading part.

For the Arapahos and the Cheyennes, the most important ceremony of the year was the Sun Dance. In this dance, an Indian tortured himself to show the tribe his bravery, and bring visions to himself and to the other dancers who were torturing themselves too. Through these visions the dancers hoped to make contact with the spirit world. They hoped to work with the spirits to make themselves better hunters or warriors, and so bring glory to the tribe.

The Indians on the Plains knew that they could not survive without the buffalo. When herds could not be found, they did not waste time going out and tracking them. Instead they performed complicated dances to try to bring themselves closer to the spirit world. They hoped that they could work with the power of the spirit world to bring the buffalo back.

SOURCE WORK: Dances

SOURCE A

A Mandan buffalo dance: a drawing by George Catlin published in 1844

SOURCE B

Black Elk describes a Sun Dance:

'The next day the dancing began, and those who were going to take part were ready, for they had been fasting and purifying themselves in the sweat lodges, and praying. First, their bodies were painted by the holy men. Then each would lay down beneath the tree as though he were dead, and the holy man would cut a place in his back or chest, so that a strip of rawhide, fastened to the top of the tree, could be pushed through the flesh and tied. Then the man would get up and dance to the drums, leaning on the rawhide strip as long as he could stand the pain or until the flesh tore . . .'

(Black Elk, in J. Neihardt, *Black Elk Speaks*)

Look at Source A and read Source B.
1 Buffalo were of vital importance to the Plains Indians: without them they would not survive. Why, then, did the Arapahos and the Cheyennes, both Plains Indian tribes, hold the Sun Dance as their most important dance?

2 Plains Indians were skilled in tracking and hunting buffalo. Can you explain why they would spend time taking part in a Buffalo Dance when they could be tracking down the missing buffalo herds?

The Plains Indians and the buffalo

Life was not easy for the Plains Indians. They lived close to nature, travelling long distances in freezing winds in winter and under the scorching sun in the summer. Even so, their free and roaming way of life was deeply important to them. Everything in their lives came from the fact they were nomadic – that they did not live in settled communities, but wandered from place to place, setting up camp wherever they happened to stop whilst they followed the herds of buffalo.

Hunting the buffalo

As soon as they had horses, the Plains Indians did not have to stalk the buffalo on foot, covered in wolf skins, or wait for a herd to crash into a trap. They still, from time to time, chased a herd towards a cliff, where the buffalo tumbled to their deaths. But this was just for fun. Nothing could match the excitement of hunting the buffalo on horseback in a thrilling and skilful chase.

George Grinnell, a scientist who lived with the Indians for a while, took part in a buffalo hunt in 1872. After this he wrote:

'It is sad to see so much death, but the people must have food, and none of this meat would be wasted.'

Nothing, indeed, was wasted. The buffalo which the Indians hunted and killed supplied nearly everything which they needed. The buffalo was so important to the Plains Indians that Francis Parkman, who made an extraordinary journey through Indian country in the 1840s, wrote in his book, *The Oregon Trail*, 'When the buffalo are extinct, the Indian too must dwindle away'.

Francis Parkman's words were to be all too true. However, for the moment let us see how the Indians used this animal upon which their whole life depended.

A painting of an Indian hunting buffalo by Rosa Bonheur, 1889

The uses of the buffalo

When the buffalo had been brought back to the camp, the parts which were good to eat raw, like the kidneys, the liver and the brain, were cut out first by the women. The flesh was boiled or roasted before eating. Anything left over was sliced into thin strips and smoked or dried in the sun. This 'jerky', as it was called, would keep for a long time and would help to feed the tribe during the cold winter months. The women also made pemmican from left over meat. They would pound the meat until it was pulp, mix it with berries and pour in into skin containers.

Once hot grease and marrowfat had been poured over, the container would be airtight and the pemmican would keep for a very long time.

Even the dung of the animals was used – as fuel. The rough part of the tongue came in handy as a hairbrush!

The buffalo hide, as you can see from the picture below, had many uses. But the one part of the buffalo which was never used was the heart. This did not mean that it was not important. It was cut from the dead animal and left on the Plains to give new life to the herd which had given the Indians the buffalo which they needed so much.

This shows all the different ways in which Indians used the buffalo

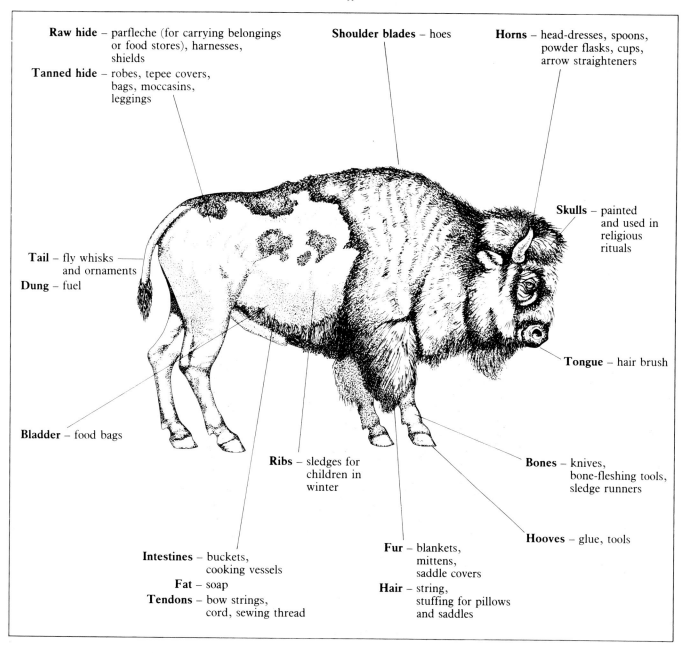

Raw hide – parfleche (for carrying belongings or food stores), harnesses, shields

Tanned hide – robes, tepee covers, bags, moccasins, leggings

Shoulder blades – hoes

Horns – head-dresses, spoons, powder flasks, cups, arrow straighteners

Skulls – painted and used in religious rituals

Tail – fly whisks and ornaments

Dung – fuel

Tongue – hair brush

Bladder – food bags

Ribs – sledges for children in winter

Bones – knives, bone-fleshing tools, sledge runners

Hooves – glue, tools

Intestines – buckets, cooking vessels

Fat – soap

Tendons – bow strings, cord, sewing thread

Fur – blankets, mittens, saddle covers

Hair – string, stuffing for pillows and saddles

SOURCE WORK: The buffalo

SOURCE A

'Then the crier shouted like singing:
    "Your knives shall be sharpened. Make ready, make haste; your horses make ready!
    We shall go forth with arrows. Plenty of meat we shall make!"
Everybody began sharpening knives and arrows and getting the best horses ready for the great making of meat. Then we started for where the bison were.'
    (Black Elk, in J. Neihardt, *Black Elk Speaks*)

SOURCE B

'At once all were on their feet. For a moment they gazed bewildered at the dark line that was sweeping toward them, and then, down went every huge head and up flew every little tail, and the herd was off in headlong stampede for the opposite hills. The oldest man of the Indians turned back towards us and uttered a shrill "Loo-ah"; it was the word we had waited for.
    Like an arrow from a bow each horse darted forward. . . . What had been only a wild gallop became a mad race. Each rider hoped to be the first to reach the top of the opposite ridge, and to turn the buffalo back into the valley. . . . How swift those little ponies were, and how admirably the Indians managed to get out of them all their speed! I had not gone more than half way across the valley when I saw the leading Indians pass the head of the herd, and begin to turn the buffalo. Back came the herd, and I soon found myself in the midst of a throng of buffalo, horses and Indians. There was no yelling and shouting on the part of the men, but their stern, set faces, and the fierce gleam of their eyes, told of the fires of excitement that they were burning within them. It was far more interesting to watch the scene than to take part in it, and I soon rode to a little knoll from which I could overlook the whole plain. Many brown bodies lay stretched upon the ground, and many more were dashing here and there attended by relentless pursuers.'
    (G. Grinnell, *When the Buffalo Ran*, Yale University Press 1920)

SOURCE C

'The buffalo supplies them with the necessaries of life; with habitations, food, clothing, beds and fuel, strings for their bows, glue, thread, cordage, trail ropes for their horses, covering for their saddles, vessels to hold water, boats to cross streams, and the means of purchasing all they want from traders.'
    (F. Parkman, *The Oregon Trail*, Lancer Books 1968)

1 Sources A and B describe a buffalo hunt. Read them carefully.
   a) Explain whether you agree or disagree with the following statements:
      i) Indians had to hunt buffalo so often that they found buffalo hunts very boring.
      ii) Buffalo hunts were carefully planned beforehand.
      iii) Indians found hunting buffalo more exciting than killing them.
   b) Now read Source C. How does this source help to explain sources A and B?
   c) Why do you think that George Grinnell (Source B) found it more interesting to watch a buffalo hunt than to take part in it?

2 Look at Source D opposite.
   a) Explain carefully whether or not George Catlin has painted a buffalo hunt which was the same as that which George Grinnell described (Source C).
   b) What *new* information is this picture giving you?
   c) How does this source help you to understand the importance of the buffalo to the Indians?

SOURCE D

A buffalo chase in winter: a painting by George Catlin, 1841

SOURCE E

'When the butchering was all over, they hung the meat across the horses' backs and fastened it with strips of fresh bison hide. On the way back to the village all the hunting horses were loaded, and we little boys who could not wait for the feast helped ourselves to all the raw liver we wanted. Nobody got cross when we did this. . . .

During this time, women back at the camp were cutting long poles and forked sticks to make drying racks for the meat. When the hunters got home they threw their meat in piles on the leaves of trees. . . . The women were all busy cutting the red meat into strips and hanging it on the racks to dry. You could see the red meat hanging everywhere. The people feasted all night long and danced and sang. Those were happy times.'

(Black Elk, in J. Neihardt, *Black Elk Speaks*)

SOURCE F

'The squaws flung down the load from the burdened horses, and vast piles of meat and hides were soon gathered before every lodge. By this time it was darkening fast, and the whole village was illumined by the glare of fires. All the squaws and children were gathered about the piles of meat, exploring them in search of the daintiest portions. Some of these they roasted on stocks before the fires, but they often dispensed with this operation. Late into the night the fires were still glowing upon the groups of feasters engaged in this savage banquet around them.'

(F. Parkman, *The Oregon Trail*)

3 Black Elk (E) and Francis Parkman (F) both described what happened after a buffalo hunt.
   a) On what points do the sources *agree*?
   b) On what points do the sources *disagree*?
   c) Both Black Elk and Francis Parkman were describing something they had seen. Which of the following suggestions *best* explains the differences between their accounts?
      i) Francis Parkman would not really know or understand what was going on because he was a white man.
      ii) Black Elk and Francis Parkman were describing different tribes.
      iii) Black Elk had forgotten what had really happened, as he was an old man when he told this story.
      iv) There was no particular custom about who unloaded the meat.

4 Use the sources and your own knowledge to explain which animals were more important to the Plains Indians – horses or buffalo.

The tepee

Buffalo provided the Plains Indians with their homes. The tepee was the home of each Indian family. It was a tent with a frame of wooden poles arranged in a circle and covered with between ten and twenty buffalo hides, sewn together. In winter a fire in the middle of the tepee helped to keep the family warm and to cook their food. The smoke from the fire went out of the hole at the top of the tepee. There were flaps which could be adjusted according to the direction of the wind, so that smoke blew away and not back down into the tepee. The Indians decorated their tepees inside and out with brightly coloured paintings of animals and birds, or with geometric designs. They put rugs on the floor, and on top of these put comfortable cushions made of skins and stuffed with a soft filling.

Colonel Dodge, a white man who travelled for many years among the Plains Indians, wrote about the tepee:

> 'In this small space are often crowded eight or ten persons, possibly of three or four different families. Since the cooking, eating, living and sleeping are all done in the one room, it soon become inconceivably filthy.'

A contemporary drawing of a tepee by Karl Bodmer

Chief Flying Hawk, of the Oglala Sioux, would not have agreed with him. 'The tepee . . . is always clean, warm in winter, cool in summer', he wrote.

It is perhaps not surprising that the white man is just a little critical of life in a tepee. Colonel Dodge did go on to admire the design of the tepee and the fact that it could be kept warm in winter with very little fuel. The way in which the Indians lived in the tepee, though, must have seemed strange to someone used to living in a house.

Karl Bodmer was a Swiss artist who began a journey across the Plains in 1833. At the time he was the official artist for a German prince, Maximilian of Wied Neuwied, who was touring the USA. Bodmer was a trained artist who recorded detail carefully and accurately. This is one reason why his pictures of the American West are particularly useful. Look carefully at the picture below of a tepee which belonged to Indians of the Assiniboin tribe.

It would have been too dangerous for an Indian family to live alone on the Great Plains. They put up their tepees, sometimes called lodges, close to those of other Indians.

George Catlin's painting of a Comanche village, 1830s

Indians on the move

The Plains Indians needed to follow the vast herds of buffalo which roamed the Plains. This meant that their lodges were always being taken down and put up again somewhere else. When the Indians moved camp, of course, they had to take absolutely everything with them. They used travois to carry all their possessions. Travois were made from two tepee poles, joined at the horses' shoulders. The other ends trailed on the ground. In the middle of the poles the Indians would put a frame or a net for carrying their belongings. Seth Eastman's painting on page 22 shows what these looked like.

You have seen how the coming of the horse changed the Plains Indians' way of life. It even changed the size of their tepee. Before the horse, the Indians used their dogs to help them. Dogs could only pull a fairly small and light travois. Tepee poles were used to make the travois, and therefore these had to be small. If tepee poles were small, then so was the tepee! Horses, however, could pull heavier loads, which meant that the poles could be longer and the tepee could be bigger. However, no matter how long the poles or heavy the load, Indians had to be prepared to move camp very quickly indeed.

SOURCE WORK: Indians on the move

SOURCE A

'The lodges are taken down in a few minutes by the squaws and easily transported to any part of the country where they wish to encamp. They generally move six to eight times in the summer, following the immense herds of buffalo. The manner in which an encampment of Indians strike their tents and transport them is curious. I saw an encampment of Sioux, consisting of six hundred lodges, struck and all things packed and on the move in a very few minutes. The chief sends his runners through the village a few hours before they are to start, announcing his determination to move, and the hour fixed upon. At the time announced, the lodge of the chief is seen flapping in the wind, a part of the poles having been taken out from under it; this is the signal, and in one minute six hundred of them were flat upon the ground.'

(G. Catlin, *North American Indians: 1*)

1 Source A describes the way in which an Indian camp was taken down.
  a) How important was the chief in dismantling the camp?
  b) How important were the squaws in dismantling the camp?
  c) In your judgement, did the squaws or the chief play the more important part?

2 Use your own knowledge as well as Source A to explain:
  a) Why it was so important to be quick when dismantling a camp;
  b) Why George Catlin, who had lived among the Indians, described the way in which they dismantled their camp, and the way in which they travelled, as 'curious'.

3 Look back at the picture on page 21. Since it was important to be quick when dismantling a camp, why did the Comanches put their tepees so close together?

SOURCE B

Seth Eastman's painting of travelling Indians. Seth Eastman (1808–75) was a US army officer who had a great interest in the West and Indians in particular. He was appointed as illustrator for the Office of Indian Affairs and produced 300 paintings for a book: Indian Tribes of the United States

SOURCE C

Henry Boller, who lived among the Plains Indians for some years in the middle of the nineteenth century, wrote:

'The long poles used in pitching the lodges were carried by the horses, fastened by the heavier end, two or three on each side, to a rude sort of pack saddle, while the other end drags on the ground. About a foot behind the horse, a kind of basket is suspended between the poles and firmly lashed in its place. On the back of the horse are piled various articles of luggage; the basket is also filled with domestic utensils, or, quite as often, with a litter of puppies, a brood of small children, or an old man. Numbers of these curious vehicles [*travois*] were now splashing together through the stream. Among them swam countless dogs, often burdened with miniature travois themselves. Dashing forward on horseback through the throng came the warriors, the slender figure of some lynx-eyed boy clinging fast behind them. The women sat perched on the pack-saddles, adding not a little to the load of the already overburdened horses. The confusion was tremendous. The dogs yelled and howled in chorus; the puppies in the travois set up a dismal whine as the water invaded their comfortable retreat; the little black-eyed children, from one year of age upward, clung fast with both hands to the edge of their basket.'

(H. A. Boller *Among the Indians: Eight Years in the Far West*, University of Nebraska Press 1972)

4 Source B shows an Indian band on the move. Source C describes an Indian band on the move. Is it the same Indian band? Explain your answer.

5 As you can see in Sources B, C and D, travelling does not seem to have been very comfortable for the Indians!
  a) Why, then, did they travel over the Plains at all?
  b) Why did they choose to travel in this particular way?

SOURCE D

A modern photograph of Indians on the move with a travois

Family life

Bands, tribes and nations

An Indian family, as you have seen, lived together in its own tepee. However, if you look back at the pictures on pages 20 and 21, you will not see a tepee standing alone by itself. All families who were related to each other would pitch their tepees together and travel together in a group called a band. All the different bands in a tribe would usually meet together in the summer for a great tribal camp, when the grass was rich enough to feed all the buffalo they would need. Some tribes were part of a larger group called a nation. The Oglala Sioux and the Teton Sioux, for example, were all part of the Sioux nation.

Children

Francis Parkman stayed with the Oglala Sioux Chief Big Crow and his family. He reported that:

'Both he and his squaw, like most other Indians, were very fond of their children, whom they indulged to excess and never punished, except in extreme cases, when they threw a bowl of cold water over them.'

Francis Parkman seems to think that the Indians spoiled their children. Big Crow would probably not agree. The Indian way of bringing up children was very different from the way in which Francis Parkman would have been brought up. It was all to do with the different ways in which Indians and white people looked at the world. In particular it was to do with the Indians' respect for all living creatures.

Children were taught, from a very young age, to respect all living things. The mother earth and everything which lived on her had a dignity and importance of their own. This is shown in the way in which children were taught to be polite to their elders at all times. They were not so spoiled that they were allowed to be rude and speak disrespectfully to older members of their band and tribe.

The Sioux nation

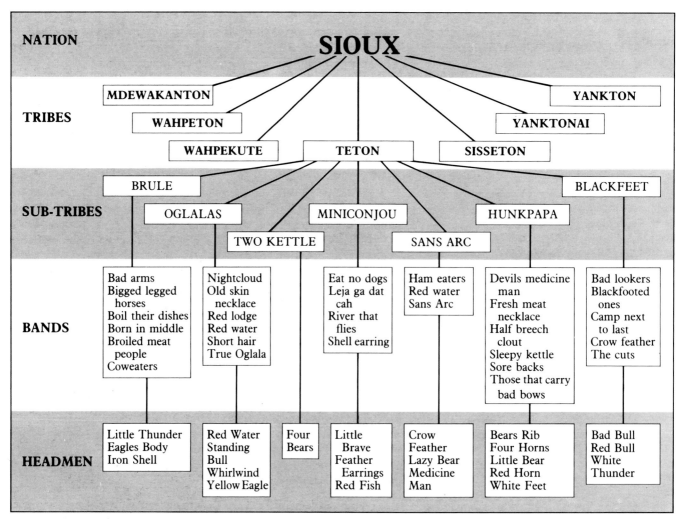

All members of the family were important to each other, and, living in a band in which most of the people were related to each other, children would never be without someone to look after them. Aunts and uncles would look after nephews and nieces if their parents died, and cousins were always treated like brothers and sisters.

As children got older, their families prepared them for the different parts they would have to play when they were adults. A boy would learn the skills of a warrior – war and horsemanship. A girl would learn how to put up and take down a tepee, and how to cut up and prepare buffalo to provide food and clothing for the family.

Marriage and divorce

Many tribes regarded the jobs of the men and of the women in a family as being equally important. Men had the job of defending the band against enemies, whether two or four footed. However, once the band was safe, it was the women who made day-to-day living possible. It was the women of the band who put up and took down the tepee, and who had to see that these and all the family's possessions were loaded on to the travois when they moved camp. It was the women who butchered the buffalo and prepared them for use. In some tribes, the tepees belonged to the women. A young man, in such a tribe, would move in with his new wife's family when he married.

Not all Indian marriages were happy. 'I throw her away!' Simply by beating a drum and shouting these words a Cheyenne could divorce his wife. The men, however, did not have it all their own way. There were some tribes in which women played a very important part, and where everything – tepee, utensils, tools, children – belonged to the woman. When a man from one of these tribes wanted to divorce his wife he had to leave everything except the clothes he was wearing, and go back to his mother's tepee.

Widows and old people

Nomadic people, who have to fight for their survival, depend on the strength of the band to protect them against their enemies. They have to think of the safety of the whole band as well as of the individuals within it. As a result the Indians had some customs which seem strange to us today. If men were killed in hunting or in war, their widows were shared out and married to the surviving men, even if the men had wives already. This helped the women – and the men – because one wife could not usually do all the work which was necessary for a growing Indian family. The man had to protect the women, and look after the surviving children. They were his responsibility as well as the responsibility of the whole band. This custom also made certain that all women of childbearing age did, in fact, have as many children as possible. This way the tribe increased in numbers and strength.

Old people were a big problem to tribes which were always on the move. They became too ill or too tired or too weak to keep up with their band. Many old Indians used to take matters into their own hands, and go off by themselves to die. Others would insist that the band leave them behind when they moved camp.

This woodcut by Frederic Remington shows a young Indian boy learning how to break a pony. Frederic Remington had a great deal of knowledge about the West. He first travelled there in 1880. He had an exciting life, as a cowboy, a prospector for gold, and a traveller. He followed the Oregon and Santa Fe Trails, and visited various Indian settlements in his travels over the Plains and the mountains

SOURCE WORK: Family life

SOURCE A

'Throwing-Them-Off-Their-Horses is a battle all but the killing. Sometimes they got hurt. The horsebacks from the different bands would line up and charge upon each other, yelling; and when the ponies came together on the run, they would rear and flounder and scream in a big dust, and the riders would seize each other, wrestling until one side had lost all its men, for those who fell upon the ground were counted dead.'

(Black Elk, in J. Neihardt, *Black Elk Speaks*)

1 Children played an important part in the life of the tribe. Look back at page 24 and read again the section on children. Francis Parkman tells us that Indians did not punish their children very strictly. Do you think that this was because:
   a) Indian parents did not care how their children grew up?
   b) Indians believed that all living things were important and should be respected?
   c) The Indian ways of bringing up children were not as good as the ways of white people?

2 Games can be fun, but they can have a serious side too. Use Source A to help you explain why Indian children played games.

SOURCE B

'The son of this chief, a youth of eighteen years, distinguished himself by taking four wives in one day! This . . . was just the thing to make him the greatest sort of medicine in the eyes of his people. Wishing to connect himself with some of the most influential men in the tribe, he held an interview with one of the most distinguished, and made an arrangement for the hand of his daughter, for which he was given two horses, a gun, and several pounds of tobacco. He soon made similar arrangements with three other leading men of the tribe.

I visited the wigwam [*tepee*] of this young medicine man several times, and saw his four little wives seated round the fire, where all were entering very happily on the duties and pleasures of married life. The ages of these young brides were probably all between 12 and 15 years.

In this country polygamy [*having more than one wife at a time*] is allowed; and in this tribe where there are two or three times the number of women than there are of men, such an arrangement answers a good purpose; for so many females are taken care of.'

(G. Catlin, *North American Indians: 1*)

SOURCE C

'To support several women, of course, requires greater effort on the part of the man in hunting, but this is more than made up for in their work in dressing skins. This enables the man to buy horses, guns and other means to hunt more easily. When buffalo are plenty, anyone can kill. The rawhide of the animal has no value. It is the work of putting it into the form of a robe or a skin fit for sale or use which makes it valuable. Women therefore are the greatest wealth an Indian possesses next to his horses. Often they are of primary consideration as after war their labour is the only way he can acquire horses, the only standard of their wealth.'

(Adapted from the diary of Edward Denig, an American trader writing in the middle of the nineteenth century)

3 Use Sources B and C and your own knowledge to explain what Indian marriage and divorce tell us about the importance of women to the tribe.

4 Read Sources B and C carefully.
   a) What reasons does George Catlin give for Indian men having more than one wife at a time?
   b) What *additional* reasons does Edward Denig give for Indian polygamy?
   c) George Catlin and Edward Denig were very unlikely to have approved of polygamy for themselves or for their neighbours back home. Why, then, did they approve of polygamy for the Indians?

SOURCE D

'When we were about to start on our way from the village, my attention was directed to a very aged and emaciated man, who was to be left to starve.

His friends and his children were preparing in a little time to be on the march. He had told them to leave him.

"My children", said he, "our nation is poor, and it is necessary that you should all go to the country where you can get meat. My strength is no more, my days are nearly numbered, and I am a burden to my children. I cannot go, and wish to die."

This cruel custom of exposing their aged people belongs to all the tribes who roam about the prairies, making severe marches, when such old people are totally unable to ride or walk. It often became absolutely necessary in such cases that they should be left; and they always insist on it, as this old man did.'

(G. Catlin, *North American Indians: 1*)

SOURCE E

'We travelled at a rapid pace, and an old lame Assiniboine Indian, who had been living with his family among the Gros Ventres during the winter and who was looking forward to returning to his people, found it very difficult to hobble along fast enough.

He had one horse and a travois, upon which his three children and all his worldly goods were transported. His squaw led the wretched animal and the old Indian toiled painfully along in the rear. He used such exertions to keep up that the perspiration rolled in streams down his . . . countenance [*face*], even though the morning was cold. All his efforts, however, were in vain and he was finally left behind, loudly protesting against being abandoned in such a dangerous country and so far from his people's camp.'

(Adapted from H. A. Boller, *Among the Indians*)

5 Read Source D carefully.
   a) What reasons does the old Indian give for being willing to be left behind by his family to die of exposure?

   b) How does George Catlin explain the Indian custom of exposure?

6 Now read Source E.
   a) In what ways does the story Henry Boller tells differ from that told by George Catlin?
   b) How can this difference be explained, when both the writers had lived among the Indians and knew them well?

7 George Catlin has explained why the Indian men had more than one wife at a time. He seems to approve of the custom. He has also explained why the Indians left their elderly and infirm relatives behind to die of exposure when they travelled over the Great Plains. He does not, however, seem to approve of this custom, as he calls it 'cruel'.

   Can you suggest why he should feel so differently about these two customs?

SOURCE F

'A squaw with three small children was also left. She carried one on her back and another in her arms, while the eldest trotted along by her side. Some time after, a young Indian who had loitered behind came up and reported that the squaw had just killed the youngest because it was too small to travel.'

(Adapted from H. A. Boller, *Among the Indians*)

8 Look back at page 24 of this chapter, and read again the section on children. Now read Source F.

   Indians, as you have seen, were supposed to love their children dearly and respect every living thing. Why, then, did this squaw kill her youngest child?

Government of the band and the tribe

We have seen that the tribes did not move about together, but were divided into bands of closely related families. These, you might think, would have had some way of keeping law and order. They did. Everything was controlled by custom and tradition. People hated to do wrong, because if they did, they would be badly thought of and publicly shamed. It was not until white people came to the Indian lands that the Indians needed the word 'law'.

The Council

The real government of the tribe was in the hands of a council of leading men from each band, who were usually peace chiefs. (In some tribes there were different chiefs for war and peace.) Chiefs did not order, they offered advice, and the voice of the chief would not be listened to any more than that of any other respected member of the tribe. No decision could be made until every man at the Council had agreed to it. It was during the meetings of the Council that the ceremonial smoking of a pipe took place. The Indians believed that the smoke from the pipe would carry their words and their desires up into the spirit world so that the spirits could help the members of the Council make wise decisions.

This photograph shows an Indian Council in 1891

A fur trader in an Indian Council lodge, drawn by Frederic Remington, 1880s

Warrior societies

Each tribe had its own warrior societies, and each man would belong to one. Every warrior society had its own special costume and dances and songs. The members would meet and talk and exchange ideas. The Blackfoot, and some other tribes, had societies which were graded by age, so that the men would move from one to another as they grew older.

One of the most famous societies was that of the Dog Soldiers of the Cheyenne. All the working men of the tribe belonged to this society. Their job was to protect. They had to protect the women and children of the tribe, and because of this it was the Dog Soldiers who gave all the orders for marches. They had, too, to protect the buffalo. This may sound strange when the buffalo were going to be killed by the Indians, but it was really a very sensible thing to do. The Dog Soldiers had to see that only just enough buffalo were killed for the tribe's needs; they also had to see that the herd was not disturbed when some buffalo were killed. This was important as the whole herd might have panicked, stampeded and disappeared.

You can read what Colonel Dodge had to say about the Dog Soldiers on page 31. He clearly thought that they were very skilful in not alarming the buffalo when some of the herd were being killed. He added that '. . . half a dozen white men would have driven them all away in a day'.

Colonel Dodge also found it difficult to understand the Indians' very loose system of government. He complained that he never found an Indian or white person who could explain it properly to him. He did say, however, that the system seemed to suit the Indians and that it worked.

Painting of a Mandan medicine man, dressed for the Dog Dance, by Karl Bodmer

SOURCE WORK: Government of the band and the tribe

SOURCE A

'When the Comanche were asked "How did you select your headmen?", answers were vague. As one man put it, "No one made him such; he just got that way".'

(E. Wallace and E. A. Hoebel, *The Comanches*, Holt, Rinehard and Winston 1954)

SOURCE B

'In a treaty either with whites or Indians of other nations, the leading chief's voice would have no additional weight because he was in that position. He would be allowed to state his opinion with others of the same standing as men in the same band, but nothing more.'

(Edward Denig, an American trader, writing in the middle of the nineteenth century)

1 Use Sources A and B, together with your knowledge of the Plains Indians, to explain whether you agree or disagree with these statements:
a) Indian laws were carefully kept by the whole tribe.
b) There was no point in becoming a chief because chiefs had no power.
c) Indian councils represented all sections of the tribe.

2 Look carefully at the painting by Seth Eastman (Source C), the photograph of the Indian Council and the drawing by Frederic Remington of the Council on page 28. Look back at the details about Remington on page 25. Look also at the details about Seth Eastman underneath the painting on page 22.
a) What conclusions can be drawn about Indian councils from these pictures?
b) How accurate would you judge these conclusions to be?

SOURCE C

An Indian Council, painted by Seth Eastman in 1849

3 Look back at the answers you wrote to question 1(b) in the Source Work section 'Indians on the move' (page 22), and to questions 3 and 4(b) in the Source Work section 'Family life' (page 26).

Clearly women had an important part to play in the life of the tribe. Why, then, were there no squaws on the Indian councils?

SOURCE D

'Because no good thing can be done by man alone, I will first make an offering and send a voice to the Spirit of the World, that it may help me to be true. See, I fill this sacred pipe with the bark of red willow. These four ribbons hanging here on the stem are the four quarters of the universe. The black one is for the west where the thunder beings live to send us rain; the white one for the north, from whence comes the great white cleansing wind; the red one for the east, whence springs the light and where the morning star lives to give men wisdom; the yellow for the south, whence comes the summer and power to grow. And because it means all this, and more than any man can understand, the pipe is holy.'

(Black Elk, in J. Neihardt, *Black Elk Speaks*)

SOURCE E

'All these peoples and all these things of the universe are joined to you who smoke the pipe – all send their voices to Waken Tanka, the Great Spirit. When you pray with this pipe you pray for and with everything'.

(Sioux legend)

4 Read sources D and E. Why did Indians rely on magic and not their own knowledge, experience and judgement when they had to make decisions?

SOURCE F

'Whatever the power of the chief and council there is another power to which both have to yield. This power is the hunters of the tribe, who form a sort of guild. Among the Cheyennes these men are called 'Dog Soldiers'.

This guild comprises the whole working force of the band. It is they who supply and protect the women and children. From them come all orders for marches. . . . One of the most important functions of the 'Dog Soldiers' is the protection of the game. Except when laying in the supply of meat for winter, only sufficient buffalo is killed for the current supply of the camp. Great care is taken not to alarm the herd, which will feed for days around a camp of a thousand people, while half a dozen white men would have driven them all away in day.'

(Colonel R. I. Dodge, *Hunting Grounds of the Great West*, Chatto and Windus 1877)

5 Read Source F.
a) What special skills did the Cheyenne Dog Soldiers have?
b) Look back to Source C in the Source Work section 'The Buffalo' on page 18. How does this source help to explain why the chief and the Council had to give way to the Dog Soldiers?

SOURCE G

'I cannot say exactly how the powers and duties of these three governmental forms, ie. chiefs, councils and dog-soldiers blend together. I have never met an Indian or white man who could satisfactorily explain them. The result, however, is fairly good and seems well suited to the character, necessities and peculiarities of the Plains Indians.'

(Colonel Dodge, *Hunting Grounds of the Great West*)

6 Colonel Dodge (Source G) seems fairly puzzled about the way in which the Indian tribes governed themselves. Use the sources and your own knowledge to explain:
a) which aspects of Indian government Colonel Dodge would have found the most puzzling;
b) why he would find these puzzling when he had travelled among the Indians for so long.

Warfare

You may go on the war-path.
When your name I hear,
Having done something brave
Then I will marry you.

(Sioux love song)

Every young Indian boy dreamed of winning glory in battle. This was, for him, the only way to earn respect. No man could become a chief until he had a record of bravery and success in war.

Unlike most white people, Indians did not go to war in order to conquer others or to gain territory. They did not want to conquer and rule over other tribes, and so they did not have to defend their own tribe against others who wanted to kill and conquer them. Indian warfare was made up of short raids, made by small groups, in order to capture horses or to kill their enemies for revenge or honour.

Horses – captured by stealth, ridden with skill

An Indian band's wealth would not be counted in the amount of land which it had, for, as you have seen, the Indians did not believe that anyone could own land. Their riches would be the horses which they owned or had stolen from other tribes. Horse stealing became a great art amongst some tribes. The Comanches were particularly skilful horse thieves, but they were also magnificent horse-riders. You have seen how young boys learned, from an early age, how to fight in war and how to handle horses. By the time they were grown-up warriors, Indians had learned to be amazingly skilful with horses, as you can see from this picture!

The young warriors enjoyed showing visitors their skills. George Catlin described the time he watched young Comanche men galloping in front of his tent, showing off on horseback. You can read his account of this on page 36. Look, too, at the painting by Frederic Remington on page 36 (Source A).

Weapons

The white man brought the Indians the horses which transformed their lives. He also brought guns, which turned those Indians who had them into even deadlier shots than they already were with bows and arrows. Indians still used their traditional weapons, though, and you can see some of these in the illustration opposite.

Counting coup

Counting coup by touching the enemy with your hand or with a specially decorated stick was the highest honour which a warrior could win, especially if his enemy was alive. In doing this he had risked his life. He had been amongst the enemy and had come back alive. The first man to touch an enemy in this way received the highest honour. There were lesser honours for those who touched the enemy second, third and fourth.

A warrior's success in warfare depended on how many times he had counted coup. A famous Crow chief had counted so many he was called Plenty Coup! Successful warriors could be spotted immediately by the feathers which they wore in their hair.

A mounted messenger brings news to camp: a woodcut made in 1881

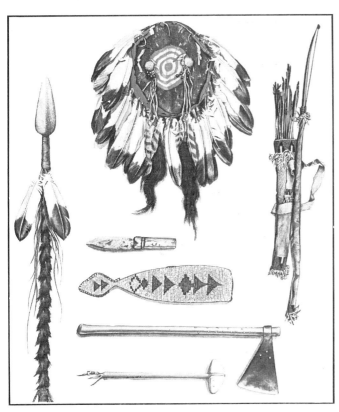

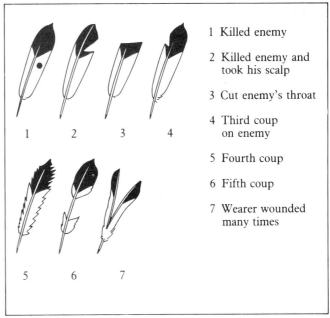

1 Killed enemy

2 Killed enemy and took his scalp

3 Cut enemy's throat

4 Third coup on enemy

5 Fourth coup

6 Fifth coup

7 Wearer wounded many times

Above: *The meaning of different feathers*

Left: *Traditional Indian weapons*

Below: *Remington's painting of counting coup, 1880s*

The Indians' idea of bravery

The Plains Indians would not have understood the way in which the white man fought battles. The white man was expected to stand and fight until the last man was dead. The Indian gained honour when he touched an enemy. A white man would probably have felt that this showed no bravery at all. An Indian warrior did not want to die. What a waste that would be! Why risk being killed when he could slip away and live to fight another day!

Scalping

There was another reason for the Indians' desire to avoid death in battle – fear of being scalped. Being scalped was one of the very worst things which could happen to an Indian. If your enemy had your scalp, he also had your spirit. That would prevent it from going to the Happy Hunting Ground. In much the same way, an Indian would be very careful when cutting his hair or his nails. He would always bury the cuttings secretly in case anyone else found them and gained hold of his spirit.

When an Indian killed in battle, he scalped the person and carried the scalp back to camp. Scalps were dried and displayed in many ways – on top of tepee poles, hanging from horses' bridles, sewn into the seams of a warrior's clothing. After a successful raid, there would be the Scalp Dance. The warriors and their women would leap, stamp and shout around the scalps which had been brought back. Those Indians who had lost their scalps but had survived would now be able to restore their own spirits with the scalp of a dead enemy!

An Indian scalping a dead cavalryman: an engraving of 1892

An engraving of Catlin's painting of an Indian Scalp Dance, 1840

The pipe of peace

'If this sacred symbol was taken to Sioux warriors in the thickest of battle, they would at once obey its mandate and retire.'

(Chief Luther Standing Bear)

You have seen how the Council used to smoke the pipe whilst they were making important decisions. The peace pipe was one of the Indians' most sacred possessions. It was used on all important occasions, in peace and in war. If an Indian disobeyed the command of the pipe, even in the midst of the fiercest battle, he would bring disgrace to himself and to his whole band.

The threat of change

The Plains Indians' way of life had remained unchanged for centuries – unchanged, that is, since the tribes had first acquired horses. Their way of life had remained unchanged because there was no need for change. Buffalo roamed the Great Plains in their millions – and the Plains Indians depended upon the buffalo. As long as the buffalo were there, the Indians would hunt them. As long as the Indians could hunt buffalo, their way of life would not change. But change – enormous, dramatic and violent – was to come to the Plains, and this change, as you will see, and was to end the Plains Indians' way of life for ever.

Pipe of peace

SOURCE WORK: Warfare

SOURCE A

This 1890 engraving by Frederic Remington shows a Comanche performing the trick which Catlin was describing in Source B

SOURCE B

'Amongst their feats of riding, there is one which has astonished me more than anything of the kind that I have ever seen, or expect to see, in my life. Every young man in the tribe is able to drop his body upon the side of his horse at the instant he is passing, effectually screened from his enemies' weapons as he lies in a horizontal position behind the body of his horse, with his heel hanging over the horse's back, by which he had the power of throwing himself up again, and changing to the other side of the horse if necessary. In this wonderful condition, he will hang whilst his horse is at the fullest speed, carrying with him his bow and his shield, and also his long lance of fourteen feet in length.

This astonishing feat which the young men have been repeatedly playing off to our surprise as well as our amusement, whilst they have been galloping about in front of our tents, completely puzzled the whole of us, and appeared to be the result of magic, rather than of skill acquired by practice.'

(G. Catlin, *North American Indians: 2*)

SOURCE C

'War has been transformed into a great game in which scoring against the enemy often takes precedence over killing him. The scoring is in the counting of coup – touching or striking an enemy with hand or weapons. Coups counted within an enemy encampment rank the highest of all. . . . A man's rank as a warrior depends on two factors: his total "score" in coups, and his ability to lead successful raids in which Cheyenne losses are low. Actual killing and scalping get their credit, too, but they do not rate as highly as the show-off deeds.'

(E. A Hoebel, *The Cheyenne*, Holt, Rinehart and Winston 1978)

1 In Source B George Catlin describes a very skilful horseback trick developed by the Comanche Indians. Frederic Remington has painted the same trick (Source A).

Use your knowledge of the Indians, together with Sources A and C, to explain when the Indians would be most likely to use this trick.

SOURCE D

'Men and horses were all mixed up and fighting in the water. Then we were out of the river, and people were stripping dead soldiers and putting the clothes on themselves. There was a soldier on the ground and he was still kicking. A Dakota rode up to me and said: "Boy, get off and scalp him."

I got off and started to do it. He had short hair and my knife was not very sharp. He ground his teeth, and then I shot him in the forehead and got his scalp.

I thought I would show my mother the scalp, so I rode over towards the hill where there was a crowd of women and children. When I got to the women on the hill they were all singing and making the tremolo [*a high-pitched vibrating noise, made with the voice*] to cheer the men fighting across the river in the dust on the hill. My mother gave a big tremolo just for me when she saw my first scalp.'

(Black Elk in J. Neihardt, *Black Elk Speaks*)

SOURCE E

'The Comanche warrior out to count coup had no wish to die in battle, for he had to guard his immortal soul. He wanted horses, he desired plunder, and he would take women and children captive if he could, but he did not want to die. To die in battle was to risk scalping, and a scalped warrior could not enter heaven . . . . Courage was the highest virtue among the Comanche, and they exhibited extraordinary courage when they carried off the bodies of their dead; but once a warrior's scalp had been taken, not even the bravest Comanche would touch the corpse.'

(Odie B. Faulk, *The Crimson Desert* Oxford University Press 1974)

SOURCE F

'The Indians' idea of the future life in the Happy Hunting Ground is vague. All persons who die unscalped will meet in that final heaven. He goes there with the same wishes and needs. He will meet enemies whom, however, he strives to make as few as possible in that world by scalping as many as possible in this.'

(Colonel Dodge, *Hunting Grounds of the Great West*)

2 In Source D Black Elk described the first time he scalped anyone.
   a) Why was his mother so pleased with what he had done?
   b) How do Sources E and F help to explain why it was important that
      i) enemies were scalped?
      ii) Indians did all they could to avoid being scalped?

SOURCE G

'The concept of bravery was completely different from that of the Europeans who came to live in the region. The Comanche thought it stupid to stand and fight when there was no chance of winning anything save honor; instead they would slink away from such a contest, to return another day to steal horses, booty and captives.'

(Odie B. Faulk, *The Crimson Desert*)

3 a) Use the sources in this section and your own knowledge of the Plains Indians to explain which of these actions an Indian would have thought brave:
      i) Wild Crow galloped furiously into the enemy camp when the last arrow had been fired. He touched Chief Still Waters with his coup stick as he lay dead in front of his tepee.
      ii) Grey Raven refused to leave his lodge and follow his band to the safety of the hills when the Cheyenne attacked. Though heavily outnumbered, he fought fiercely until he was killed defending his own home.
      iii) Black Eagle slid into the enemy camp late at night. He trod silently until he reached the tepee of Chief Hard Foot. Carefully he cut the hide rope which bound the horses to the sleeping men inside, and made off with his prizes.
   b) Which sources did you use to help you make up your mind?
   c) Which of these actions (i, ii or iii) would *you* have thought brave?
   Do your ideas of bravery and those of the Indians agree? Why do you think this is?

EARLY SETTLERS IN THE WEST

Mountain men

Mountain men and Indians

In 1890 Frederic Remington drew the picture below of two mountain men and added the caption 'I took ye for an Injun'. It is easy to see why he did this. The mountain man on the right does look very much like one of the Indians you have been reading about in Chapter 2. The similarities did not stop there. Mountain men like Jim Bridger, whom you will read about again later in this chapter, were expert hunters and trackers. Some of them married Indian women. Like the Indians, the mountain men knew about the ways of animals and the uses of plants. Sometimes they worked with Indians, sometimes they fought them.

A mountain man called Osborne Russell kept a journal between 1834 and 1843. He tells here of one occasion when things went badly wrong:

'We were completely surounded. We cocked our rifles and started thro' their ranks into the woods which seemed completely filled with Blackfeet. An arrow struck White on the right hip joint. I hastily told him to pull it out and as I spoke another arrow

'I took ye for an Injun'

struck me in the same place. At length another arrow striking thro' my right leg above the knee benumbed the flesh so that I fell across a log. . . . I . . . kept hopping from log to log thro' a shower of arrows. . . . I was very faint from loss of blood and we set down among the logs determined to kill the two foremost when they came up and then die like men. About 20 of them passed by us within 15 feet without casting a glance towards us and all turning to the right the next minute were out of our sight among the bushes.'

The life of a mountain man

The mountain man's job was to trap beavers and hunt other animals for their fur. Most of them worked for trading companies like the Rocky Mountain Fur Company. Some worked for themselves, however, selling their furs and skins wherever they could get the best prices. They roamed the Sierra Nevada and the Rocky Mountains which bordered the Great Plains, setting their traps and getting to know every rock and waterfall, forest and swamp, pass and canyon. They saw the fertile plains and rich soils of Oregon and California beyond the Rockies.

Mountain men faced danger every day as they trapped and hunted wild animals. They also had to face hunger and thirst, freezing cold and intense heat. There were other dangers, too. Jedidiah Smith, the leader of a group of mountain men, had his scalp and ear torn off by a grizzly bear. One of the group, called James Clyman, described in his diary how they coped with the massive wound:

'None of us having any surgical knowledge what was to be done one Said come take hold and he would say why not you so it went round I asked the Capt. what was best he said one or two go for water and if you have needle and thread git it out and sew up my wounds round my head. [This I did] laying the lacerated parts [of the ear] together as nice as I could with my hands. This gave us a lisson on the character of the grissily Bare which we did not forget.'

Every year between 1815 and 1840, mountain men, trappers, traders and Indians held an enormous gathering called a Rendezvous, where they would buy and sell furs. It was here that the mountain men talked of adventure and warned of dangers. They also told of the rich, fertile lands which lay beyond the Rocky Mountains and which were simply waiting for people to settle there and farm.

The importance of the mountain men

This news of good farming land west of the Rockies was told and re-told by traders travelling up and down the Missouri River. It was spread eastwards among the farmers of Missouri, Mississippi, Ohio and Illinois. It was news that was to change the lives of thousands of people. Many mountain men became guides to those who travelled west. They used their knowledge of the Great Plains, Rocky Mountains and Sierra Nevada to lead the early settlers safely into Oregon and California.

SOURCE WORK: Mountain men

SOURCE A

'I cast my eyes down the mountain and discovered two Indians approaching within 200 yards of us. I immediately aroused my companion, who was still sleeping. We grasped our guns. They [the Indians] quickly accosted us in the Snake tongue saying they were Shoshonies and friends to the whites. I invited them to approach and sit down, and then gave them some meat and tobacco. After our visitors had eaten and smoked, they pointed out the place where we could descend the mountain.'

(Osborne Russell's Journal 1834–43 in J. Chandler, *The Settlement of the American West*, Oxford University Press 1971)

1 Read Source A and then read the other extract from Osborne Russell's Journal on page 38. These sources seem to give very different accounts of the ways in which mountain men and Indians behaved toward each other.
   a) Which of these statements gives the more likely explanation of the difference between the accounts?
      i) Osborne Russell had changed his ideas about Indians between writing the two entries in his Journal.
      ii) The Shoshonis were a peaceful tribe and the Blackfeet were not.
      iii) One of the sources is wrong.
   b) In both these sources, the mountain men were the first to have their guns ready. Mountain men, therefore, seem to have been more suspicious of Indians than Indians were of mountain men.
      Use the two pictures by Frederic Remington on pages 28 and 38, together with any other information you have, to explain why this may have been so.

2 Look again at the picture 'I Took Ye For An Injun' on page 38.
   a) If the mountain men were so distrustful of the Indians, why did they want to look like them? (Look again at the picture of the mountain man in the Indian Council lodge on page 28.)
   b) Why were these Indians not afraid to allow a mountain man inside their council lodge?
   c) Would you agree that the mountain men needed the co-operation of the Indians more than the Indians needed the co-operation of the mountain men?

SOURCE B

'Jim Bridger is one of the hardy race of mountain men who are now disappearing from the continent, being enclosed in a wave of civilisation. With a buffalo skin and a piece of charcoal, he will map out any portion of this immense region, and delineate [draw] mountains, streams, and the circular valleys called "holes" with wonderful accuracy.'

(An account by an army surveyor sent to the West in the 1840s to map it more scientifically, in J. Chandler, *The Settlement of the American West*)

3 Read Source B carefully.
   a) Were the maps produced by Jim Bridger likely to be less accurate than the maps drawn by the army surveyor?
   b) One of the ways in which Jim Bridger put his skills to good use was in guiding the wagon trains to Oregon and California. Was this the only real importance of the mountain men in the story of the settlement of the West?

Migrants: pioneers go to the far West

The first pioneers

Between 1839 and the end of the 1850s thousands of men, women and children deserted their homes in the East, leaving everything and nearly everyone they knew. They packed what they thought they needed into wagons and hand-carts, and began a difficult and dangerous journey across land which was totally unknown to them. Many people did not survive; others suffered terribly and kept the scars of the journey all their lives. What made them do it?

You have read of the mountain men and their stories of rich, fertile land beyond the Sierra Nevada. You have seen that the mountain men had a unique understanding and knowledge of those mountains, and were willing to lead parties through to the other side. You know, too, that the American Government wanted to settle the West before emigrants from other countries did so. But the men and women living at the time didn't know this. They could not be certain that the land beyond the Rockies was rich and fertile. They did not know whether the mountain men were to be trusted. There were no television documentaries about farming west of the Rockies. There were no roving correspondents travelling with the wagon trains, and no satellite weather maps of the western coast line. All that the early migrants had were stories handed on by word of mouth. Men and women would not have risked all that they had, and faced the dangers of the unknown, unless conditions at home in the East were becoming so dreadful that nothing could be worse.

In 1837 a financial crisis hit eastern America, making thousands of people bankrupt and leaving many more without a job. However, financial crises come and go, and many people may have hoped that things would, in time, improve.

At the same time, though, farmers who wanted their own land in the East were being disappointed. There were simply too many of them trying to buy land in the same area. In Missouri, for example, the population grew from 14,000 in 1830 to 353,000 in 1840. When land was scarce, and people were terribly short of money, stories of fertile, empty lands in Oregon and California must have seemed very attractive. Their grandparents and great-grandparents had crossed the Appalachian mountains to farm the

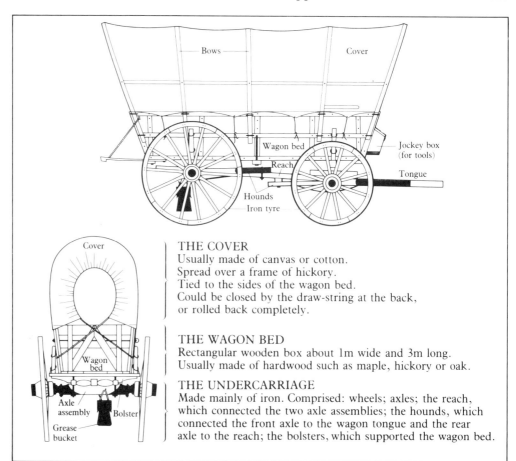

This was the type of wagon most often used to cross the Plains

Bows — Cover

Wagon bed

Jockey box (for tools)

Reach

Tongue

Hounds

Iron tyre

Cover

Wagon bed

Axle assembly — Bolster

Grease bucket

THE COVER
Usually made of canvas or cotton.
Spread over a frame of hickory.
Tied to the sides of the wagon bed.
Could be closed by the draw-string at the back, or rolled back completely.

THE WAGON BED
Rectangular wooden box about 1m wide and 3m long.
Usually made of hardwood such as maple, hickory or oak.

THE UNDERCARRIAGE
Made mainly of iron. Comprised: wheels; axles; the reach, which connected the two axle assemblies; the hounds, which connected the front axle to the wagon tongue and the rear axle to the reach; the bolsters, which supported the wagon bed.

empty, fertile lands in Missouri and Arkansas; they, in their turn, would go west and cross the great Plains and Rocky Mountains to the rich, lush lands beyond. So it was that the first pioneers left for Oregon in 1839, and for California in 1840. By 1850, which was the peak year for emigration, some 55,000 people had travelled west.

Wagons and wagon trails

Nowadays, when we move house, we might get a furniture removal firm to pack up our possessions and move them for us. We might hire a large van and do it ourselves. Not many people would choose to put all that they had in a wooden cart measuring just over 1 metre wide by just over 3 metres long, and then get a horse or bullock to pull it. Yet this is just what the pioneers did.

These wagons were very important to the pioneers. They had to protect the migrant families and their possessions from the weather. They had to be homes and storehouses, hospitals and fortresses as well. Not all wagons were equal to the task. In 1841, 1843 and 1844, for example, no wagons reached California. Their owners had abandoned them in the Rockies. They put what they could on to the horses and fled, afraid of being trapped in the mountains by the deep snows of winter.

In the early days the first pioneers found their own way west with the help, in the final stages, of the mountain men. Before very long, however, there were several well worn, tried and trusted trails. The most popular ones were the California Trail and the Oregon Trail. The fact, however, that these routes were well known did not, as you will see, mean that they were easy or even safe.

Trails westward across the Plains

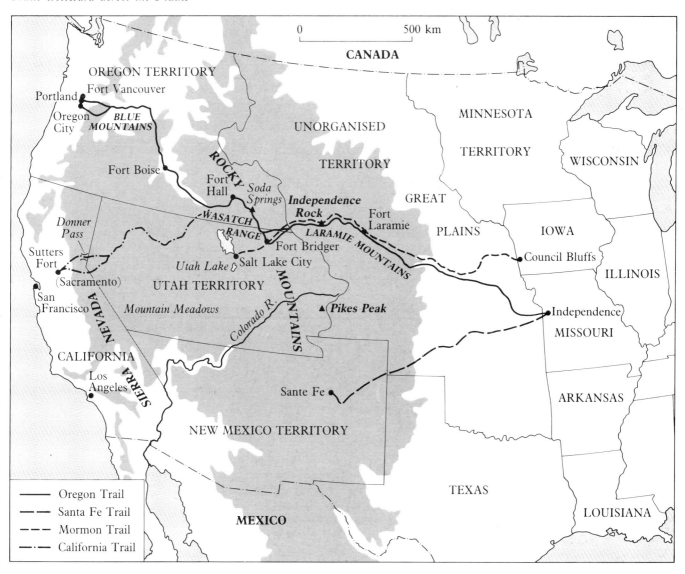

Preparing for the journey west

Independence, a town on the border of Missouri, became very important to the pioneers. Here they made final decisions about what to take with them, checked their wagons and took on supplies. Here, too, they formed up into wagon trains, hoping to make the journey into the unknown as safe as possible. The size of the wagon trains varied. It depended on such things as the number of strong young men in the group, and the particular skills which a group had. You would not, for example, want to leave Independence without a skilled hunter in your party.

Not many trains had fewer than twenty wagons. One of the largest groups set out in 1843 with 1000 men, women and children, 120 wagons and several thousand horses and cattle. Sometimes wagon trains would stay for many days in Independence. They would be waiting for just the right time when the prairie grass was rich enough and sweet enough to feed the animals. Then they would not have to take up valuable space by carting animal food with them.

Few realised just how hard the journey would be. Jesse Applegate, one of the early pioneers, wrote:

Emigrant families by their wagons

'Once started on the journey, the problem was to finish. We didn't think much about the unborn generations who would profit by our venturesomeness. It was simply a desperate undertaking.'

Dangers and disasters

According to official estimates 34,000 people died on the westward trails between 1840 and 1860. This was nearly eleven people for each kilometre of the journey. The Plains and mountains tested the pioneers in quite different ways. On the Plains, the wagons crawled along, covering perhaps 20 kilometres a day. The pioneers faced sandstorms and rain, hunger and thirst, quicksands and swollen rivers, stampeding buffalo and, sometimes, hostile Indians. There was, too, another enemy – disease – as this extract from the diary of a pioneer tells us:

'But another enemy, unseen and without one audible word of demand or threat was at that very hour advancing upon us, and made our wagon his first point of attack. That enemy was cholera.'

When they reached the Rockies the pioneers would be weakened from their experiences on the Plains.

Journey's end: more than thirty horses pull a combine harvester through an Oregon wheatfield in the early 1880s

However, there was no time to rest. They had to push and pull wagons and possessions, children and animals through the high, narrow passes in the mountains. Here there was always the worry that the weather would close in on them and the autumn snows would come too soon, leaving them trapped in the Rockies or the Sierra Nevada. This happened to a group of migrants led by George Donner, who left Independence in 1846.

The forty adults and forty-one children who made up the Donner party were very well equipped. They had horses, oxen, cattle, wagons, money and luxuries like built-in beds and fancy foods. However, they made every mistake possible. Their first mistake was to leave Independence late in the year, after the other wagon trains had already left. Then they tried to catch up on lost time by leaving the marked trail and taking an untried short cut. In late October 1846 they were trapped in deep snow on the wrong side of the Sierra Nevada. They decided to stay where they were and make camp for the winter. Conditions quickly became appalling. Animals died, food ran out, and men, women and children were weak and close to starvation.

A small group of fifteen adults, including two Indian guides, decided to try to battle through drifts and blizzards on foot to California to get help for the others. The small amount of food they took with them quickly ran out. After a few days four of the men were frozen to death in a snowstorm. The little group survived only because they roasted and ate their dead friends. The two Indian guides died later and were eaten too. The survivors finally reached the safety of an Indian village after thirty-two days.

Word quickly spread, and a rescue operation began

to try to reach the trapped Donner party. Four separate groups set out from California. They risked their own lives struggling through blizzards and deep snows carrying packs of food for the men, women and children whom they hoped to find alive. They did find some. They had survived by eating those of their group who had died of starvation. Eighty-one people had set out from Independence with high hopes, but only forty-seven eventually made it through to California.

Journey's end

For most pioneers, however, the journey had a happier conclusion. Nathaniel Ford, reaching Oregon in 1844, wrote in a letter home:

'We had a tedious and tiring trip: but I think we are well paid for our trouble; we are in the best country I have ever seen for farming and stock raising. The prairies are easily broken with two yoke of oxen, and harrows up fine for seeding. All the springs and streams are cool and fine flavoured.'

Once in Oregon and California the pioneers settled down to the kind of farming they had been used to in the East. To them the Great Plains had been an enormous and terrifying obstacle. They had shown great courage in making the journey across the unknown and dangerous to land which was safe and familiar, and which they knew they could farm well. It was the Homesteaders, as you will read later, who were to show even greater courage in settling on the Great Plains, painfully and slowly turning them into prosperous farmland.

SOURCE WORK: Migrants

SOURCE A

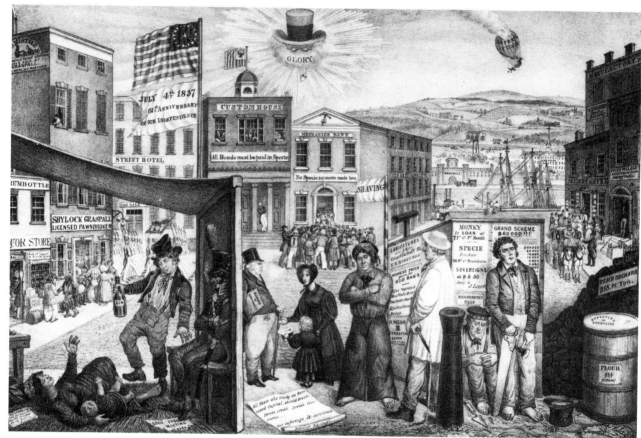

A cartoon from The Times, *New York, on the financial problems of 1837*

1 Look carefully at Source A.
   a) List all the troubles it shows.
   b) How could the early pioneers be sure that they would not find these troubles waiting for them in Oregon and California?
   c) How far does this source help to explain why people travelled west?

SOURCE B

This extract is from a letter written in 1845 by a twenty-six-year-old Oregon settler, Medorem Crawford, to his brothers in the eastern states.

'Oregon City, June 28th 1845
Dear Brothers John and Ronald,
Doctor White is going home with the intention of returning to this country with his family

and a band of cattle. So if indeed he should not alter his mind, and should indeed come back, the door is opened for one or both of you to come to Oregon. But you must not start off with less than 75 dollars apiece, which . . . will afford you with about 25 or 30 dollars on hand when you arrive at Independence.

If you arrive at Independence before the party are ready to start, apply yourselves to some kind of business among the farmers to get cattle. Do not fail to secure a few head of heifers from $1\frac{1}{2}$ to 2 years old or perhaps what would be better would be a young cow with a heifer calf some 2 months old. . . . You should if possible get each a good young mule well broke to ride and a Spanish saddle, bridle and spurs.'

(H. Horn, *The Pioneers*, Time Life 1974)

2 Read Source B carefully.
a) Explain whether you agree or disagree with these statements:
  i) The trail to Oregon must have been dangerous because Medorem Crawford suggested that his brothers travelled with Dr White and his family.
  ii) Medorem Crawford and Dr White were both successful and prosperous settlers.
  iii) Cows could not be bought in Oregon.
b) Use your knowledge of the journey to Oregon to say how sensible Medorem Crawford's advice was.
c) How important would letters like this be in persuading people to join friends and relations who had made the journey west to Oregon and California?

SOURCE C

These are extracts from the diary of Amelia Knight. She and her husband left Iowa in 1853 for Oregon. They took with them their seven children – Plutarch, Seneca, Frances, Jefferson, Lucy, Almira and Chatfield.

'Made our beds down in the wet and mud. . . . Cold and cloudy this morning and everybody out of humour [cross]. Seneca is half sick. Plutarch has broke his saddle girth. Husband is scolding . . . and Almira says she wished she was at home, and I say ditto [the same]. . . .

We are creeping along slowly, one wagon after another . . . and the same thing over, out of one mud hole and into another all day. . . . It has been raining all day long. The men and boys are all soaking wet and look sad and comfortless. The little ones and myself are shut up in the wagon from the rain. Take us all together we are a poor looking set, and all this for Oregon.

Chatfield, the rascal, fell under the wagon. Somehow he kept from under the wheels. I never was so frightened in my life. I supposed Frances was taking care of him.

Chatfield quite sick with scarlet fever. A calf took sick and died before breakfast.

Here we left, unknowingly, our Lucy behind. Not a soul had missed her until we had gone some miles when we stopped a while to rest the cattle; just then another train drove up behind us, with Lucy. It was a lesson to all of us.

Lost one of our oxen; he dropped dead in the yoke. I could hardly help shedding tears.

Passed a sleepless night as a good many of the Indians camped around us were drunk and noisy.

I was sick all night and not able to get out of the wagon in the morning . . . . Yesterday my eighth child was born.'

(H. Horn, *The Pioneers*)

SOURCE D

This extract is from a letter written by John Marsh, an early migrant, to several newspapers. It is dated 3 July 1840.

'The difficulty of coming here is imaginary. The route I would recommend, is from Independence to the hunter's rendezvous on Green River . . . thence to the Soda Spring on Bear River, above the Big Salt Lake, thence to Portneuf, thence to Mary's River, down Mary's River until you come in sight of the gap in the great mountain, through that gap by a good road . . . and you arrive in the Plain of Joaquin, and down that river on a level plain through thousands of Elk and horses, three or four days journey and you come to my house.'

(H. Horn, *The Pioneers*)

3 Read Sources C and D, and look again at the description, on page 43, of what happened to the Donner party when they tried to get to California. All describe wagon journeys westward. All the journeys were made over similar routes and using the same sort of transport.
a) Why, then, were the experiences of the pioneers on the journeys described in Sources C and D so different?
b) If these journeys were so terrible, why did people go west at all?

4 Look at the picture on page 43. Does it prove that the pioneers were right to decide to move west?

The Mormons: a special group of migrants

The migrants from the East, struggling to cross plains and mountains, relied very much on the wisdom and advice of the mountain men. This was because, as you have seen, the mountain men knew the land over which the migrants were travelling, and could help them to avoid many dangers. Not everyone, however, followed the advice of the mountain men.

Mormons and the mountain men

In 1847 the mountain man, Jim Bridger, and two of his friends were travelling along a deserted trail which led, eventually, to the desolate wastes of the Great Salt Lake. As they journeyed they saw, coming towards them, a small group of men who were clearly the advance party of a much larger group. Their leader was a man called Brigham Young. Jim Bridger was horrified when he learned that Brigham Young was planning to lead a much larger group of men, women and children across the Great Plains to settle in the infertile wasteland around the Great Salt Lake. Desperately he tried to persuade Brigham Young to change his mind, and to choose instead the rich farmlands of Oregon. Brigham Young refused.

Finally, Jim Bridger made a promise: he would give Brigham Young a thousand dollars for the first bushel of grain raised in the valley of the Great Salt Lake. A thousand dollars was a lot of money in those days, and Jim Bridger must have felt that it wasn't very likely that he would have to pay up. Still Brigham Young refused to change his mind. So the two men walked away from each other, Jim Bridger to give advice to those who would listen, and Brigham Young to come to grips with the work of settling people in arid, infertile land.

Perhaps Brigham Young wasn't altogether surprised when Jim Bridger tried to persuade him to go to Oregon – to go anywhere, in fact, which wasn't near to the Great Salt Lake. One of Brigham Young's group, William Clayton, wrote about a trapper called Mr Harris who shared Jim Bridger's views:

'Mr Harris says he is well acquainted with the Bear River Valley and the region around the Salt Lake. From his description which is very discouraging, we have little chance to hope for moderately good country anywhere in those regions. He speaks of the whole region being sandy, and destitute of timber and vegetation except the wild sage.'

Indeed, one of Brigham Young's own group, Sam Brannan, who sailed around Cape Horn to California, and then travelled east across the Rockies to meet him, brought the same message:

'For Heaven's sake don't stop in this God forsaken land. Nobody on earth wants it. Come to California, to a land of sunshine and flowers.'

Why did Brigham Young ignore such good advice? Why did he choose to try to make a living from poor, arid land? Why, indeed did he choose to settle far away from any of the other migrants, and on land so poor that no-one, apart from those in his own group, would want to settle close by?

Joseph Smith

In order to answer these questions, we have to go back to 1823, and to a place called Palmyra in New York State. Joseph Smith, the son of a poor farmer, claimed that he had dug up a set of gold plates from the mountainside near to his home. Joseph said that an angel called Moroni had told him what to do. Four years later, Moroni allowed Joseph Smith to translate the mysterious signs and symbols on these gold plates. Then a strange tale was revealed. It told of battles in America between the tribes of Israel, beginning before the birth of Jesus Christ, and ending long after His death. Mormon and his son Moroni were two survivors of these terrible battles. They wrote down, on golden plates, all that had happened to them. They said that whoever found the plates would restore the church of Jesus Christ in America, and build up God's kingdom on earth in readiness for Christ's second coming. It was, as you have seen, Joseph Smith who had found the plates.

What a fantastic story! But was it true? Only Joseph Smith actually saw these golden plates and read the story which was written on them. The plates were so special, and so secret, that Joseph had to be extra careful when he was translating them. He strung a blanket across the room in which he was working, and sat on one side of it with the golden plates. He then called out the translation to his wife and to some friends who sat on the other side of the blanket and who wrote everything down. Finally, in March 1830, Joseph Smith was able to publish *The Book of Mormon*. A year later he had over a thousand followers: the Mormons.

There were many religious sects, or groups, in America, but right from the start the Mormons were different. They believed that if they gave God their complete obedience He would choose them to be His special people in Heaven and on earth. No one else but Mormons would be chosen, because it was only to Joseph Smith whom God had sent His angel Moroni. And it was only the Mormons who had the golden plates which told them what they had to do to build Christ's kingdom on earth.

Kirtland

The building of this kingdom had to start somewhere, and in 1831 Joseph Smith chose the city of Kirtland in the state of Ohio. This was to be 'Zion', the Heavenly City. Mormons flocked there in their thousands. The Mormons bought land for farming and built homes in the city. Soon there were more Mormons living in Kirtland than the non-Mormons who had been there in the first place.

Then in 1833 the Mormons began building an enormous temple so that they could worship together. The Mormon Church became involved more and more in the economic life of Kirtland. They set up a Mormon bank, which was open to non-Mormons as well as to Mormons. Mormons were encouraged to dedicate their land and property to the Mormon Church, and to hand over to the bishops all the profits they made. These profits were then invested in Mormon and non-Mormon businesses.

This led to quarrels between Mormons, and between Mormons and non-Mormons. Sometimes these quarrels could be very violent. They reached a peak in 1837, when Kirtland was hit by the financial crisis which you read about on page 40. The Mormon bank failed, as did many other banks and businesses in Kirtland. A great deal of money was lost by a great many people.

The Mormons were angry with their leaders who had given them bad financial advice, and who had failed to realise that such a serious crisis was coming. Their anger was nothing, however, compared with the fury of the non-Mormons who had lost money. Of course, many non-Mormon enterprises failed as well. But the Mormons had told everyone that they were God's chosen people. Non-Mormons had therefore invested in Mormon enterprises because they thought that they would never fail. It is not really surprising, therefore, that when things went wrong, they blamed the Mormons. Joseph Smith and his Mormons were chased out of Kirtland, and were forced to flee to other Mormon settlements in Missouri.

Mormon journeys and settlements

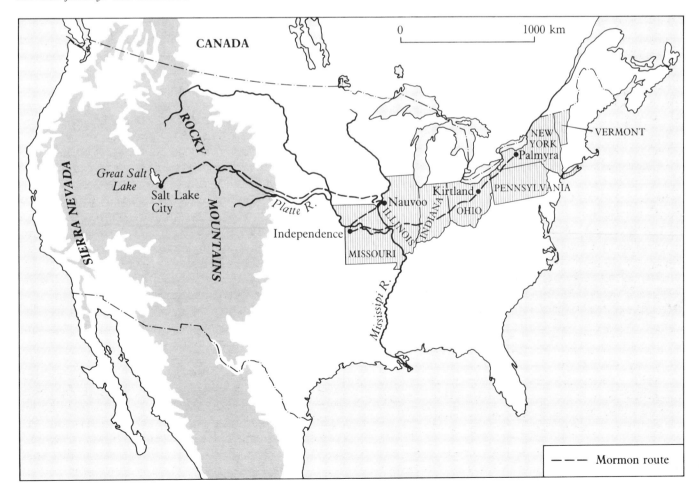

Missouri

At first the Mormons were successful in Missouri. Their experiences in Kirtland had shown them how important it was to remain together as a group in order to build God's heavenly city on earth. In Missouri they began to buy land and to farm and build. However, it was not long before the spread of Mormons into surrounding counties angered ordinary people. These people were irritated by the Mormons' hard work and carefulness. They were suspicious of Mormon land purchases, and did not believe Mormon claims that God wanted them to own the whole region. Worse still, they suspected the Mormons of being friendly with the Indians and in favour of abolishing slavery.

It was not surprising that violence broke out once again. This time, however, unlike the years in Kirtland, the Mormons organised themselves. They formed a secret organisation called the Danites. The Danites were supposed to defend Mormons against outside attackers. They also acted as a secret police for the Mormons themselves. The Mormons were determined that the problems of Kirtland would not be repeated. This determination, however, created totally new problems for the Mormons, and on a much larger scale.

Although the Danites were supposed to be a secret organisation, rumours of its existence soon spread to the non-Mormons and added to their fears. The situation was likely to become extremely dangerous. The state of Missouri ran out of patience with the Mormons, and the State Governor declared:

'The Mormons must be treated as enemies, and must be exterminated or driven from the state if necessary for the public peace.'

Most of the Mormon leaders, including Joseph Smith, were sent to gaol. By the end of November almost all the Mormons left in Missouri had fled to Illinois, led by Brigham Young, who was their only leader not in gaol.

Why Illinois? Joseph Smith would not consider a westward move because that would mean entering the terrifying wastes of the Great Plains. Six years later Joseph Smith would be dead, and Brigham Young was to make quite a different decision.

Illinois

Far from feeling defeated and downcast, their experiences in Missouri had driven the Mormons even closer together. They were even more determined to establish God's heavenly kingdom on earth.

They bought land and houses in Illinois as they had done in Kirtland and Missouri. They rebuilt the decaying town of Commerce, calling it Nauvoo, which in Hebrew means 'a beautiful plantation'. Nauvoo certainly did flourish, growing in size from 1500 inhabitants in 1842 to 11,057 in 1845. An English visitor wrote in 1843:

'Although unfinished, [Nauvoo] is of great dimensions laid out in beautiful order [with] handsome stores, large mansions and fine cottages. The inhabitants are a wonderfully enterprising people.'

Was this, then, to be Zion, the heavenly city?

The events in Kirtland and Missouri had convinced Joseph Smith that Mormons would only be safe if they held political power. Luckily both the main political parties in Illinois wanted Mormon support. Consequently, the Mormons were able to obtain a Charter which established Nauvoo as an independent city state. They had their own city council, and were able to make their own laws, as long as they did not go against the laws of the United States. The Charter also allowed the Mormons to form a private army. By 1842 this numbered 2000 men, with Joseph Smith, by now released from prison in Missouri, as their Lieutenant-General.

The dream of Mormon independence seemed to have become a reality. Would it last? Was Nauvoo to be Zion, or would the Mormons have to move on yet again?

The Mormons had established a state within the state of Illinois, and ordinary people began to be afraid. They were afraid of the power of the Mormons and of the Mormon army. They grew even more afraid when they found out that Mormon men could have more than one wife at the same time. This is known as polygamy. Non-Mormons were very shocked by this. They were also very afraid of a Mormon population explosion. Many Mormons, too, believed that polygamy was wrong. They said openly that the Book of Mormon did not allow it. They became upset and angry when they discovered that Joseph Smith himself had more than one wife. Some of them set up a break-away church because of this.

The situation was already explosive. It became even worse when one of the political parties stopped supporting the Mormons because of polygamy. When Joseph Smith announced his decision to stand for election as President of the USA all non-Mormons were alarmed.

The surrounding countryside prepared for war against the Mormons. Joseph Smith was thrown into prison. Even his death in June 1844 at the hands of the mob did not end anti-Mormon feeling. The

A cartoon from the 1840s making fun of polygamy

Charter which had given independence to Nauvoo was withdrawn, and the State Governor advised all Mormons to leave the state of Illinois.

The decision to move west

So Zion was not to be built to the east of the Great Plains, nor was it to be built to their west, beyond the Rocky Mountains in Oregon or California. Brigham Young, the new leader of the Mormons, made the decision that Zion was to be built on the other side of the Great Plains, in the desolate and deserted foothills of the Rockies, on lands surrounding the Great Salt Lake.

The early pioneers made the long and hard trek westwards because they themselves chose to go. The Mormons went west because they were forced to do so. Most ordinary people could not accept the Mormons because they thought and behaved in ways which were quite different from their own. The Mormons believed that God had chosen them alone to build His heavenly city on earth; they believed in their own rightness; they believed that they should be separate from ordinary people; Mormons supported Indians and slaves; many Mormons believed that they should be allowed to have more than one wife at the same time. It might have been possible for ordinary people to live peacefully with a religious group which held one of these beliefs. The Mormons held them all. It was these beliefs and practices which, taken together, turned ordinary people against the Mormons.

Their beliefs would not have mattered to the outside world if the Mormons had been a small group of men and women struggling to survive in some remote part of the United States. The Mormons were not. They were noisy and successful. They farmed well and bought more and more land; their businesses prospered (except during the financial crash of 1837 which affected everyone); they were even allowed to create a state within a state and to form their own private army. Added to all this, their practice of polygamy meant that more babies could be born to Mormon families because each man had more than one wife. Ordinary people feared that the Mormon population would grow at an enormous rate, eventually swamping everyone else.

It was not surprising, therefore, that the Mormons were driven from Ohio, driven from Missouri and driven from Illinois. This pattern might so easily have gone on and on repeating itself in all the eastern states of America. It was Brigham Young who had the courage to make the decision that the Mormons should build their Zion far away from ordinary men and women, and on land which no-one else could possibly want.

The journey

The Mormons had to leave Nauvoo in a hurry. This meant that they were not able to spend as much time as other migrants in thinking, planning and preparing for the long and difficult journey which lay ahead of them. They spent the winter of 1845 making what preparations they could. However, in the following spring, mobs began looting their homes and workshops, stealing and destroying their wagons and equipment. The Mormons had no choice but to leave immediately, with their preparations unfinished.

Other migrants, as we have seen, prepared well for the long and difficult journey west, but even they met with unexpected disasters. The Mormons, on the other hand, were poorly prepared. Other travellers to the west, once they had crossed the Great Plains and Rocky mountains, settled on rich farming lands. The Mormons, once they had crossed the Great Plains, were faced with dry, poor land from which to make a living. It didn't seem very likely that they would succeed. However, the Mormons had three enormous advantages which the other migrants did not have. They had had earlier experiences of moving all that they had and beginning again somewhere else; they had learned to live and to work together as a group; they had Brigham Young as their leader.

Brigham Young

You have seen already how Brigham Young was part of an advance party which travelled ahead of the main group of Mormons. This was so that he could find the best route westwards, and could choose a place to settle. But Brigham Young did far more than this. His task was to move about 1500 men, women and children 2250 kilometres into unfamiliar, dangerous territory, and to help them survive a journey for which they were poorly prepared. To do this successfully, they had to be well organised. Brigham Young was an excellent organiser. He divided the Mormons into manageable groups, each with a leader. He insisted upon strict military discipline and routine throughout the journey. Everyone had a part to play, and knew exactly what was expected of them. Brigham Young taught the Mormons how to drive their wagons in parallel lines, and how to form up into circles at night for safety. He also set up resting posts along the route. This broke the journey up into manageable sections, and made sure that neither animals nor people became too exhausted.

On 24 June 1847, Brigham Young's advance party was following tracks made by wheel ruts. They knew that the ruts had been made by the wagons of the Donner party who had earlier met with such disaster and horror in the mountains. Would their journey end as unhappily? They reached the top of a pass. There in front of them, stretching as far as they could see, were the deep blue waters of the sterile Great Salt Lake.

'We could not refrain from a shout of joy', wrote Owen Pratt, one of the advance party, in his diary. Brigham Young is supposed to have said 'It is enough. This is the right place. Drive on.' However, his sister-in-law Harriet, arriving a few days later, felt very differently.

'My feelings were such as I could not describe. Everything looked gloomy and I felt heart sick. Weak and weary as I am, I would rather go a thousand miles farther than remain in such a desolate and forsaken spot as this.'

The Salt Lake Valley: survival or prosperity?

Brigham Young led the Mormons safely to the valley of the Great Salt Lake. They arrived in groups, as he had planned. By the end of May 1848 Salt Lake City had a population of 1500 people, and ten other settlements were being established in the valley. However, to arrive was not the end of the story. In many ways the Mormons' problems and difficulties were just beginning. Brigham Young was going to need all his powers of leadership and organisation if the Mormons were to survive and flourish.

First the land on which they had settled had to be shared fairly between the Mormons. This was quickly settled by Brigham Young, who declared:

'No man can ever buy land here, for no one has any land to sell. But every man shall have his land measured out to him, which he must cultivate in order to keep it.'

If the Mormons were to survive they would have to grow crops as quickly as possible. However, the soil, although it looked rich, was very, very dry. Clearly the Lake could not provide the vital water, because it was so salty. The few streams which were there did not flow through everyone's land. Again, it was Brigham Young who decided:

'There shall be no private ownership of the streams that come out of the canyons, nor the timber that grows on the hills. These belong to the people: all the people.'

The Mormons set up a committee to plan and dig irrigation ditches, and to see that no one took more water than they needed.

Brigham Young's decision that the land belonged to everyone meant that the Church Leaders could control how much each family was allowed to farm. It also meant that they could control the building of Salt Lake City, and decide how much land was to be given to shops and houses, the Temple and Meeting Place, and other public buildings.

This is from part of a report on Salt Lake City, written by Captain Howard Stansbury in 1850:

'Through the city itself flows an unfailing stream of pure, sweet water, which, by an ingenious [clever] method of irrigation, is . . . led into every garden spot, spreading life, and beauty over what was . . . a barren waste. . . . The houses are built, principally of adobe [sun dried brick] which . . . makes a warm, comfortable dwelling.'

SOURCE WORK: The Mormons before settling in Salt Lake City

SOURCE A

Joseph Smith's account of trouble in Missouri:

'We made large purchases of land, our farms teemed with plenty, and peace and happiness was enjoyed throughout our neighbourhood. But as we could not associate with our neighbours (who were many of them the basest of men and had fled from the face of civilised society to the frontier country to escape the hand of justice) in their midnight revels, their sabbath breaking, horse racing and gambling, they commenced at first to ridicule us and then to persecute us. Finally an organised mob assembled and burned our houses, tarred and feathered, and whipped many of our brethren, and finally drove them from their habitations [homes].

This proceeding was winked at [ignored] by the government, and although we had deeds [legal documents] for our land and had violated [broken] no law, we could obtain no redress.'
(W. Mulder and A. R. Mortensen, Amongst the Mormons, Alfred A. Knopf 1958)

SOURCE B

'But little more than two years ago, some two or three of these people made their appearance on the Upper Missouri and they now number some 1200 souls in this country. Each autumn and spring pours forth its swarm among us, flooding us with the very dregs. . . .

Well grounded complaints have been already made of their corrupting influence on our slaves. . . .

One of the means resorted to by them, in order to drive us to emigrate, is an invitation to the free brethren of colour [free slaves] in Illinois to come . . . to claim the rights of citizenship.

We are told that we of this county are to be cut off, and our lands taken over by them. . . . The day is not far distant when the government of the county will be in their hands, when the sheriff, the Justices, and the county judges will be Mormons. What would be the fate of our lives and property, in the hands of jurors and witnesses who say that they have wrought miracles and supernatural cures; have conversed with [talked to] God and His angels and are fired with the prospect of gaining inheritances without price [land worth a great deal of money]?'

(Missouri Intelligencer and Boon's Lick Advertiser, 10 August 1833)

1 Read Source A.
  a) Who does Joseph Smith blame for the trouble in Missouri?
  b) What does this source tell you about Joseph Smith's attitude to non-Mormons?

2 Now read Source B and look at the cartoon about polygamy on page 49.
  a) How do these Sources help to explain why ordinary people hated and feared the Mormons?
  b) If the Mormons were as hated and feared as Source B and the cartoon on page 49 seem to suggest, why were they granted the Nauvoo Charter?
  c) Use these Sources and your own knowledge to explain whether or not you think that conflict between the ordinary people and the Mormons was bound to happen.

3 Many people opposed the Mormons. When this happened, Joseph Smith moved the Mormons to other towns which he hoped would be more friendly. Brigham Young, on the other hand, moved the Mormons to land which no one else could possibly want.

Which of these two decisions do you think was the wiser? Explain your answer.

The battle for self-sufficiency

Brigham Young knew very well how hostile many ordinary people were to the Mormons. He did not want the Mormons to have to depend upon a hostile outside world for goods which they needed. He therefore decided that the Mormons should become self-sufficient. This meant that they would produce for themselves everything they needed. This included not only food and clothing but also manufactured goods.

However, Horace Greeley, a New York journalist who crossed the Plains in 1859, tells of a series of disasters:

'Some two hundred thousand dollars was expended in preparations for iron-making at a place called Cedar City; but the ore, though rich, would not flux [*could not be made into iron*], and the enterprise had to be totally abandoned. Wood and flax can be grown here cheaply and abundantly, yet, owing to troubles last year, no spinning and weaving machinery has yet been put in operation. An attempt to grow cotton is likely to prove a failure. . . . Sugar is another necessary of life which they have had bad luck with. They can grow the beet very well, but it is said to yield little or no sugar.'

Clearly more Mormons with greater skills were needed to come and live in the Salt Lake Valley. Brigham Young therefore set up a Perpetual Emigration Fund to provide money to help poor Mormons from elsewhere in America and from Europe to make the journey. Thousands did, and gradually the Mormons became self-sufficient.

The independent Mormon state

Self-sufficiency, however, wasn't enough for Brigham Young. He wanted to make certain that the Mormons were free to follow their own customs and beliefs without outside interference. This meant that they had to be politically independent.

This was not a new idea. When the Mormons had settled in the Salt Lake Valley in 1847 it had been part of Mexico, not part of the United States. Brigham Young had hoped that the Mormons would settle quietly in this unwanted corner of Mexico, and later would be able to come to some arrangement with the Mexican government. However, to Brigham Young's horror in 1848 Mexico and the United States had fought a short, sharp war which the United States had won. This meant that large amounts of Mexican territory, including the valley of the Great Salt Lake, were handed over to the United States.

Clearly the only thing to do was to apply to be admitted to the United States as an independent Mormon state, with their own laws, their own religion and their own government. This new state was to be called 'Deseret', which means 'The Land of the Honey-bee'. The Mormons chose this name because they thought of themselves as being as busy as the worker bees.

In Washington the US Government had other ideas. All the old fears about the Mormons returned, and the Government refused to allow the Mormons to have their own state. Instead they decided to give the land the status of a territory. This meant that the Mormons could not have representatives in Washington. They would have government officials running their affairs, and the Government in Washington would always have the last word in any disputes. Furthermore, the territory was not as large as the Mormons had hoped, and did not contain a port. The Government also rejected the name of 'Deseret', and decided that the new territory was to be known as Utah, after the Ute Indians who lived there.

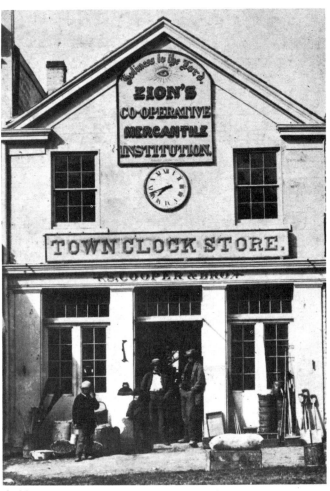

A Mormon store in Salt Lake City, 1857

A contemporary engraving of Salt Lake City in 1873

Naturally Brigham Young and the Mormons were disappointed. Their hopes for independence within the Union of the United States seemed to have come to nothing. Matters were to get worse. The United States Government appointed Brigham Young to be the first Governor of the Territory of Utah. However, the Mormons were not allowed to make their own laws. The law was administered by judges from Washington, and the territory was run by government officials. It was not surprising that there was a great deal of tension between Brigham Young and the United States Government, and that many Mormons chose to ignore the government and to keep to their own laws and practices. Reports reached Washington of government officials being insulted and even killed; of judgements made in law courts being ignored; and of Brigham Young's use of the Danites to crush all opposition from non-Mormons.

Something had to be done. Clearly Brigham Young could not allow Mormon beliefs and practices to be destroyed. Equally clearly, the Government could not allow their rule to be ignored. The Government decided, in 1857, to send a non-Mormon Governor to Salt Lake City. They sent with him 1500 troops.

The tension mounted to a fever-pitch. Bloodshed seemed inevitable. But when blood was shed, it was shed in an unexpected quarter. In September 1857 a wagon-train of 140 migrants was massacred at Mountain Meadows, some 500 kilometres to the south west of Salt Lake City. The Mormons blamed the Indians; the ordinary people blamed the Danites. Some people said that the Mormons had made a secret agreement with the Indians. No one knows for certain who was to blame. What is certain, however, is that the Mormons gained by the massacre because it changed the mind of the Government. They decided to try to get a peaceful settlement with the Mormons.

The United States Government agreed to let the Mormons live their lives in their own way. They were not, however, prepared to let the Territory of Utah become a state until the Mormon Church agreed to ban polygamy. (This happened in 1890.) In return, the Mormons agreed to accept a non-Mormon governor. However, a visitor to Utah after 1860 said:

'There is a batch of governors and judges and other officials here shipped from Washington, but Brigham Young is King.'

SOURCE WORK: The Mormons in Salt Lake City

SOURCE A

'The gardens are well filled with peach, apple and other fruit trees. Apricots and grapes are grown though not yet abundant; so of strawberries. Plums are in profusion, and the mountain currants are large, abundant and very good.

Still the average life in Utah is a hard one. The climate is severe and capricious – now intensely hot and dry, in winter cold and stormy; and although cattle are usually allowed to shift for themselves in the valleys, they are apt to resent the insult by dying. Crickets and grasshoppers swarm in myriads [*great numbers*], and often devour all before them. Wood is scarce and poor. Irrigation is laborious and expensive; as yet, it has not been found practicable to irrigate one-fourth of the arable land at all. Frost is very destructive here; Indian corn rarely escapes it wholly, and wheat often suffers from it.

I estimate that 159 days' faithful labor in Kansas will produce many of the necessities of life as 300 such days' work in Utah. Hence the adults here generally wear a toil-worn, anxious look, and many of them look older in frame [*body*] than in years.'

(H. Greeley, *An Overland Journey from New York to San Francisco, 1859*, Alfred A. Knopf 1964)

1 Read Source A and Captain Stansbury's description of Salt Lake City on page 51. Now turn back to the picture of Salt Lake City on page 53. This picture was drawn fourteen years after Horace Greeley wrote his account. The city appears to be flourishing. Does this mean that the problems outlined by Horace Greeley (Source A and page 52) had all been solved by 1873?

2 Look at the photograph of a Mormon store in Salt Lake City on page 52. The store was photographed in 1857. The Tabernacle in Salt Lake City, where the Mormons worshipped, was finished in 1871.

   Do you think, then, that trade was more important to the Mormons than religion? Explain your answer carefully.

3 Can all the credit for the success of Salt Lake City be given to Brigham Young? Use the sources in this section and your own knowledge to answer this question.

SOURCE B

President Lincoln explains his Mormon policy.

'When I was a boy on a farm in Illinois there was a great deal of timber which we had to clear away. Occasionally we would come to a log which had fallen down. It was too hard to split, too wet to burn, and too heavy to move, so we plowed around it. That's what I intend to do with the Mormons.'

(H. Horn, *The Pioneers*)

4 In Source B President Lincoln explains why the Federal Government of the United States decided to leave the Mormons alone. He is saying that the Mormons were simply too stubborn for the Government to try to change.

   Would you agree that was the reason the Federal Government, in the end, decided to let the Mormons live their lives in their own way?

5 Source C is a poster from the late nineteenth century, and is advertising a book about the Mormons.
   a) What clues can you find in the poster to help you decide whether the book is likely to be for or against the Mormons?
   b) What, according to the poster, is the author of the book trying to make his readers believe about Mormons? Why would he want to do this?
   c) Use your knowledge of the Mormons to say how accurate a picture of the Mormons is given by this poster.
   d) Would ordinary men and women
      i) be likely to buy the book?
      ii) be likely to believe what the book said about the Mormons?
   e) How useful would this source be to an historian writing about the Mormons in nineteenth-century American?

SOURCE C

This poster was advertising a book which criticised the Mormon way of life

Miners

You have seen how men, women and children made the long journey westwards because they believed they could make a better life for themselves and their families. There was, however, yet another group of people journeying westwards to California. They were not travelling with their families. Few of them crossed the Great Plains and Rocky Mountains in organised groups. Their main reason for going to California was not to settle down.

Gold rush

Early in 1848 gold was discovered in California. Quickly the news reached the eastern states and the rest of the world. Within a few months 40,000 men were reported to be crossing the Great Plains, and sixty ships carrying eager would-be-miners left ports bound for California. The gold rush had begun! Many of the men were not proper miners at all. They had had all kinds of jobs back east in offices, factories and farms, and many had no jobs at all. But they all wanted to get rich quickly. Some of them did not

A REGULAR GOLD DUSTMAN.

"Hollo! Where are you off to now?"

"Oh! I ain't a going to stop here, looking for Teaspoons in Cinders. I'm off to Kallifornier, vere there's heaps o' Gold Dust to be had for the Sweepin'."

'A regular gold dustman': a cartoon from Punch 1849

survive the journey. Most of them did not find gold and wandered back home or drifted from job to job, and from mine to mine. Some men, however, did strike gold and became extremely rich indeed. It was stories of these lucky strikes which kept men hoping that tomorrow, maybe, they would be the ones to be lucky.

Gradually, though, the gold in California which was near the surface (and therefore easy to mine) was exhausted. Then, in 1858–9, gold was discovered in the Pikes Peak region of the Rocky Mountains. Miners, and men hoping to be miners, began the great journey eastwards, back to the Rocky Mountains. Gold and silver was found in Idaho (1860), in Montana (1862), in Arizona (1863) and in the Black Hills of Dakota (1874). This last strike was to have a dramatic and terrible effect upon the Indians, which you will read about later. It is important for now to realise that the miners, having first followed the usual pattern of migrating from east to west, then, unlike the other migrants, reversed this pattern and migrated from west to east.

Miners and mining towns

Luck played an important part in the early days of the gold rush. The first miners were not really miners at all. They did not know how to mine properly, so they concentrated on looking for the loose gold near the surface. They lived in mining camps which sprung up quickly when gold was thought to be in a certain area, and which died just as quickly when the miners moved on. In the 1850s the surface gold in California was almost exhausted, and the professional miners moved in. These were men who had had training and experience in mining. Many of them had worked in the tin and gold mines of Cornwall in England, and were able to sink and work deep mines. They were backed by eastern businessmen who put money into machinery and mills, and who made gold mining a profitable industry. These professional miners built and lived in permanent mining towns, and brought their wives and families with them.

The mining towns in the Rocky Mountains and on the western edges of the Great Plains grew up quickly. They brought with them problems of law and order, which you will read about later in Chapter 7. They also speeded up the settlement of the West. The gold and silver needed to be moved quickly from the mines; the mining families needed food and manufactured goods. Not only did this mean that roads and railways had to be built, but it also meant that more and more people were attracted to the idea of moving and settling in the West.

SOURCE WORK: Miners

1 Look carefully at the cartoon on page 56 called 'A Regular Gold Dustman' published in the British magazine *Punch* in 1849. Cartoons are sometimes funny, but often have a serious point to make.
   a) What is the dustman in this cartoon hoping to do?
   b) What point was the artist trying to make when he drew the cartoon?
   c) What does a cartoon like this tell us about attitudes in England to the California Gold Rush?

SOURCE A

Gold miners exploring a cave in the Sierra Nevada, California 1859

2 a) What does this etching tell us about gold mining in California?
   b) Use the cartoon 'A Regular Gold Dustman' on page 56 and Source A, together with any other information you might have, to explain why so few men made a fortune from the gold rushes.

SOURCE B

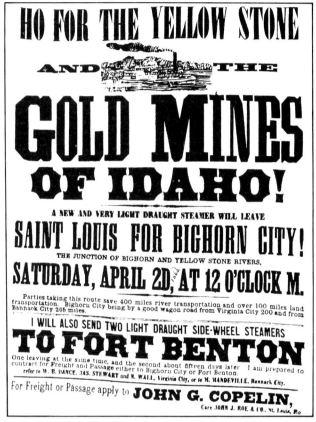

A poster of 1865 advertising travel by steamboat and wagon from the Missouri River to the gold mines of Idaho

3 Look carefully at this poster.
   a) What is John G. Copelin offering to do?
   b) What kinds of people would read the poster and take up the offer?
   c) How does this poster help you to understand what happened to gold mining in America when the surface workings were exhausted?

4 Look again at the cartoon 'A Regular Gold Dustman' on page 56, at Source A and at Source B. Which of these sources would an historian, who was trying to find out about the California Gold Rush, find the most useful?

4

THE CATTLE KINGDOM: CATTLEMEN AND COWBOYS

The Great Plains

Would white people ever settle on the Great Plains? You can see from this map, which is based on one drawn by Major Stephen Long during his expedition across the Plains in 1819–1820, that this area was described as a vast desert – the Great American Desert.

Even Colonel Richard Dodge, who was to get to know the Plains so well later, was taught when he was young that they were unknown and unexplored. He wrote this in a book which was published in 1877:

'When I was a schoolboy my map of the United States showed between the Missouri River and the Rocky Mountains a long and broad white blotch, upon which was printed in small capitals "THE GREAT AMERICAN DESERT – UNEXPLORED".'

The map which Dodge was writing about might even have been the one which you can see below.

In 1839 Thomas J. Farnham, a lawyer from Vermont (a state on the east coast of America), travelled from Illinois to Oregon. He wrote that the Great Plains region was

'burnt and a desert, whose solemn stillness is seldom broken by the tread of any other animal than the wolf or the starved and thirsty horse which bears the traveler across its wastes.'

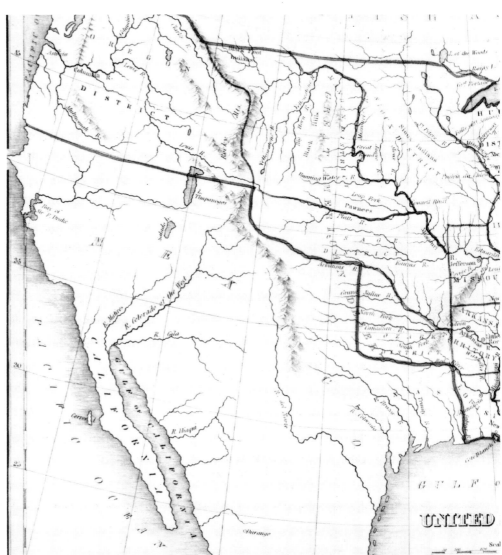

'The Great American Desert'
from T. G. Bradford's
Comprehensive Atlas, *1835*

The early pioneers crossed the Plains to find the fertile lands of Oregon and California. Here they could use their own methods of farming in lands where wood and water were plentiful. None of them thought of settling on the Plains. Anyone who attempted to do so would have to face all sorts of unknown problems and dangers. How could they raise cattle or grow crops with no water? How could they build homes or keep themselves warm in winter with no timber and no other sorts of fuel? How could they cope with sand-storms, Indians and stampeding buffalo? They would, perhaps, have to live like the Indians, by making their way of life fit in with what the Plains demanded.

The miners who had moved east in the late 1850s from California to the new gold strikes in Colorado on the western Plains had not settled or farmed the land. Only a few years after the end of the 'gold rush' many mining settlements were 'ghost towns' with deserted, broken-down shacks. The miners had come only for the gold and silver, not to become permanent settlers. Some of the small mining towns, like Denver and Colorado, were to attract settlers and later to become the big cities of the mid-West. Others, like Idaho City, became 'ghost towns'.

There were, however, to be white men who lived on and used the Plains. These were the cattlemen who owned the cattle and the cowboys who looked after them. Texas was the first home of the cattlemen and their cattle kingdom. By the mid 1870s it had spread over nearly all the states shown on the map on page 60. At first the cattle were driven over the Plains from Texas to be sold at the markets. Later, as we shall see, cattlemen decided to raise their herds on the grass of the Plains themselves. The one thing which made all this possible was the building of a railroad which connected east with west. Cattlemen realised that if they could drive their cattle north to a town on the railroad (a 'rail-head'), they could then use the railroad to reach the rapidly-growing towns of the Mid-West and the East. These towns, the cattlemen had learned, wanted as much beef as they could sell to them. We shall read about their story later. First – the coming of the railroad to the Great Plains.

SOURCE WORK: The Great American Desert

SOURCE A

'I have never seen the plains or anything like them. . . . Whoever crossed the plains at that period, notwithstanding its herds of buffalo and flocks of antelope, its wild horses, deer and fleet rabbits, could hardly fail to be impressed with its vastness and silence and the appearance everywhere of an innocent primitive existence.'

(Worthington Whittredge, *Autobiography*, ed. J. I. H. Baur, in *Brooklyn Museum Journal*, 1842)

SOURCE B

In 1806, Zebulon M. Pike set out to cross the Plains. This was his reaction:

'These vast plains of the western hemisphere may become in time as celebrated as the sandy deserts of Africa.'

(Elliot Coues, *The Expeditions of Zebulon Montgomery Pike*, Francis P. Harper 1895)

1 a) Worthington Whittredge was an artist. He also travelled over the Plains in the days of the Mountain Men. What effect did the Plains have on him?
   b) Now look back at the extract by Thomas J. Farnham on the opposite page.
      i) What *different* impression does his account give of the Plains?
      ii) These two men were writing at about the same time. Why, then, do you think that they gained these different impressions of the same place?

2 Do you think that Pike believed that people could live on the Plains? Explain your answer.

3 Now look at the map and the extract by Colonel Dodge, both on the opposite page. Use these sources and the ones which you used in Question 1 help you to think about and answer this question:
   Why did white Americans believe that no-one would ever settle on the Great Plains?

The coming of the railroad

You have read how the early pioneers crossed the Plains and the Rockies. It was a slow, dangerous and hard journey. They must have wanted very much to make the journey to have faced so many difficulties and dangers. Twenty-five years after the first trail west, the railway, or, as the Americans called it, the railroad, was to transform overland journeys. Compared with the wagon-trails it was both fast and safe. Before the 1860s all railroads, like most settlers, stopped at the Mississippi and Missouri Rivers. By 1890 railroads spanned the whole of North America.

The first railroad beyond the Mississippi-Missouri Rivers was not built to help travellers. The idea was that it should connect the industrial states of the East with the valuable land and resources of the West. It was begun in 1866. The Union Pacific railroad began at Omaha on the Missouri River, and met the Central Pacific, which began on the west coast, at Promontory Point in Utah, in May, 1869 (see the map below). The problems of building these lines were enormous.

The first problem was money. The railroad company needed money to buy land, pay the workers and buy locomotives and wagons. It also needed money to make up for the losses which would be made in the first years of operation. Very few people lived on the Plains, and so there would not be many passengers to begin with. This problem was solved, as you will see later (Chapter 5, page 76) when the Federal Government gave free land and money to the railroad companies.

The other problems were all caused by the nature of the land which the railroad had to cross: mountains, valleys, desert. All these stretched the skills of the engineers and the construction workers to the limit. Labourers died in their hundreds as the companies tried to outdo each other in the amount of track laid. If this wasn't bad enough, the labourers lived in tents in appalling conditions. They faced hostile Indians, and driving rain and snow. They bridged rivers and crossed mountains. All the time they had to depend on food brought hundreds of kilometres to them. Despite all these problems, the labourers built well, and they built fast. About 11 kilometres of track were built each day on the Plains, and the Dale Creek Bridge was built in a month. It was 38 metres high and 150 metres long. At that time, under those conditions, it was an amazing achievement.

The meeting of the Union Pacific Railroad and the Central Pacific Railroad almost didn't happen. The two railroad companies were great rivals, and, as the

The spread of cattle ranching and the first trans-continental railroad in North America

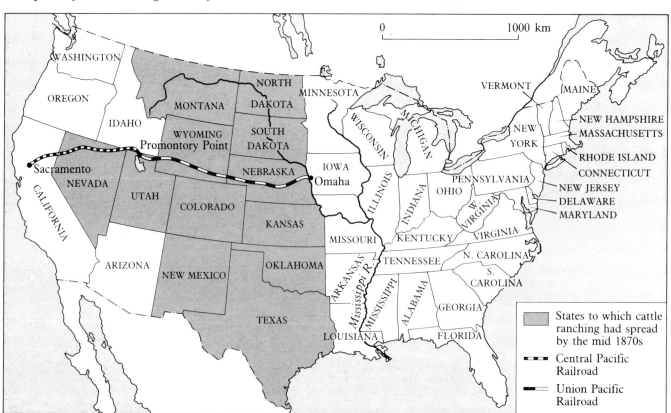

lines neared each other, they built the tracks faster and faster. The moment of meeting neared – and passed. The two crews went past each other in opposite directions. At that point the Government had to step in and ordered the lines to meet at Promontory Point. The last nail to be driven into a tie (sleeper) was made of gold, and the two locomotives were driven together nose to nose. The gold nail, of course, was removed immediately after the ceremony but that didn't alter the fact that now America had its first trans-continental railroad. Rival-

ries were buried during the celebrations when the lines met.

Other railroads were soon built on the Prairies, with the help of government grants of land and money. By 1893 there were six companies which connected the Mississippi-Missouri Rivers with the Pacific coast. The old days of the pioneers, when wagon trains struggled slowly through blizzards or blazing heat to cross the Plains and the Rockies, must have seemed very far away.

SOURCE WORK: The railroad

SOURCE A

'We had no means of fighting the snows in the Laramie Plains except by fences and sheds [*wooden covers built over the railroad to stop snow from piling up on the track*], and none were put up until the year 1870, so that when the heavy snows fell in the winter of 1869–70, it caught six of our trains west of Laramie that were snowed in there some weeks. . . . These six trains . . . were supplied with sledges and snow shoes from Laramie. They had with them, in charge of the six trains, Mr H. M. Hoxie, the Assistant Superintendant, who managed to get the trains together, but the blizzards were so many and so fierce that it was impossible for men to work out in the open. . . . Mr Hoxie handled his forces with great ability and fed and entertained his passengers in good shape. In one train was an opera company bound for California, that Mr Hoxie used to entertain the passengers with, so that when the trains reached Salt Lake City, the passengers held a meeting and passed resolutions complimentary to Mr Hoxie and the Union Pacific in bringing them safely through.'

(Maj. Gen. Grenville M. Dodge, *How We Built the Union Pacific Railway*, Sage Books 1911)

SOURCE B

Part of a poster advertising the opening of the first trans-continental railroad, 10 May 1869

1 Look at Sources A and B.
  a) The Railroad Company seems very proud to announce the opening of the railroad. Why do you think that this was?
  b) Look back at the story of the Donner party (Chapter 3, page 43), and read Source A again. What differences would the Donner party have noticed if they had been able to go by train?

2 Why was it so important to have a railroad which joined the eastern states to the west coast?

Texans on the trail

The first ranchers

The story of the cattlemen and their cattle kingdom began long before anyone dreamed of ranching on the Great Plains, and long before the railroads crossed the Plains. It is in Texas in the 1830s where we find the first cattlemen, at about the same time as the first settlers were reaching the far West. Their origins, though, lie much further back in time than this.

The Spanish conquerors of North and Central America had introduced domestic cattle and horses in the sixteenth century. The horse, as you have seen, changed forever the way of life of the Plains Indians.

The cattle which roamed the wild in these early days were the ancestors of the Texas Longhorn. These were to be the whole way of life of the Texas cowboy, and the source of the cattlemen's wealth. They were big, fierce, hardy beasts, with a thick, tough hide, usually black or dark brown in colour. The steers (males) had horns with an enormous spread of up to 1.5 metres.

The Indians who lived in what is now Texas were friendly, so the Spanish who settled there called it 'the land of the *tejas*', for the Spanish word for friend is *tejas*. From this came its modern name, Texas. Here, the Spanish settlers began cattle ranching, in the triangle of land between the Gulf of Mexico, the Rio Grande and the Nueces River (see map opposite).

Their cattle wandered freely over the rich, plentiful grass. The climate was mild and there was plenty of water. These conditions were ideal for breeding cattle. The wandering herds had to be rounded up from time to time, and so the Spanish ranchers employed Indians and half-breeds (people who were half Indian, half white) to do this. These *vaqueros* (from the Spanish word *vaca*, meaning cow) were skilled riders. They were expert at roping cattle with *la reata* (lariat), a rawhide (untreated animal hide) rope with a noose which could be pulled tight. All these skills were passed on to the American cowboy.

The first cattle trails

From about 1820 the Spanish rulers of Texas allowed American families to settle along the rich pasture and farming land on the banks of the Colorado River in Texas. When the Mexicans threw off Spanish rule in 1821, they took over Texas, and soon became alarmed at the large numbers of American settlers there. In 1830 the Americans, under General Sam Houston, rose up against their Mexican rulers and finally defeated them in 1836. Sam Houston became the first President of the Republic of Texas.

Most of the Mexican ranchers returned to Mexico, and the American Texans took over their cattle. They

A Mexican vaquero, as drawn by Frederic Remington for Harper's New Monthly Magazine, *July 1891*

also adopted the dress, customs and equipment of the *vaqueros*. They rounded up the Longhorns and branded them with their own marks.

The Texans decided that if they were to make any money out of all their cattle, they would have to drive them north, out of Texas. In Texas meat was plentiful but in the north there were many people who wanted large stocks of meat. The first cattle 'trails' began in 1837, when cowboys drove herds of between 300 and 1000 cattle to the markets of the cities in the south-west. In 1842 a trail was blazed to New Orleans. In 1846 1000 head of cattle were driven to Ohio. In 1850 drives began all the way west to California, and the first drive to Chicago was in 1856. None of these drives amounted to very much, though. The cattle were usually unbranded and there were no regular drives. Those which took place were disorganised and made little profit. What was going to happen to Texas cattle ranching?

Ranchers on the trails north

The Civil War between the northern states and the southern Confederate states began in 1861. You can read about the war in more detail in Chapter 5. The Civil War put an end to the early trails, for many Texans went off to fight for the Confederate armies. The Longhorns, free to roam the Texas ranges, grew enormously in number. By the end of the war in 1865 there were about five million Longhorns in Texas. There were few people to look after the herds during the war, so they became toughened by their need to survive.

The Texans returned from the war to find the herds running wild. Further north, however, the growing cities in the industrial areas needed as much beef as they could get – and they were prepared to pay for it. The Texan cattle men could get up to $40 per head, in the north, ten times the price which beef fetched in Texas. This meant huge profits! They rounded up the cattle, hired cowboys, and began the drives to the northern cities.

The route lay first by San Antonio, Austin and Fort Worth to sell the cattle to the cities of southern Arkansas and Oklahoma. This was the trail which became known as the Chisholm (or Chisum) Trail. It was named after Jesse Chisholm, a half-breed Indian trader, who is said to have been the first to lay down this route as a supply trail from Texas to Kansas during the Civil War.

The cattlemen soon realised, though, that if they drove their cattle the 800 kilometres or so north to the railroads, they could then get them to the rapidly-growing towns of the mid-West as well as to those in the East. In 1866, about 260,000 head of Texas cattle crossed the Red River, making for Sedalia, a rail-head of the Missouri-Pacific railroad. There the cattle were loaded into wagons and taken east to St Louis and then north to Chicago.

It was not all to be easy, though. When the Texans began to arrive in south-east Kansas, south Missouri and northern Arkansas, they were met by armed mobs. Many of these people were afraid of the deadly Texas fever which came from a tick carried by the Longhorns. The Longhorns themselves were immune from the fever, but it would have caused havoc amongst the cattle in these regions. Others in these mobs were cattle rustlers and robbers, who were prepared to fight and kill to get the valuable Longhorns for themselves.

Many drovers tried a route further to the west, reaching the railroad at St Joseph, Missouri, for the rail journey to Chicago. This proved to be safer and, as we shall see, the route of the future was to be to the west of Sedalia.

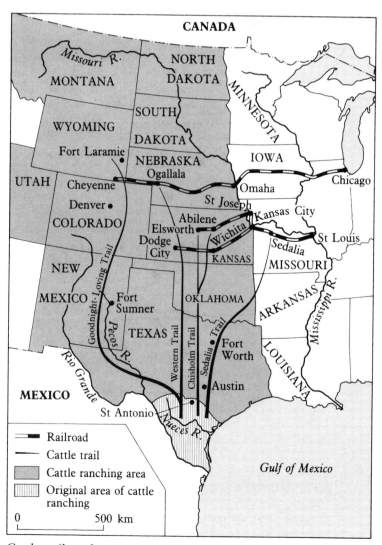

Cattle trails and cow-towns

Charles Goodnight and Oliver Loving

Charles Goodnight   Oliver Loving

The Texans who started the long drives to the North in the years after the Civil War had never thought of setting up a 'cattle kingdom' on the Plains. They were only going to market, even if that market was some 24,000 kilometres away. In the years following, though, there were to be men who set up cattle ranching on the Plains. One of these, Charles Goodnight, was also one of the most successful trail drivers.

Charles Goodnight began his cattle ranching in a way similar to many other Texans in the years just before the Civil War. He learned a cattleman's skills after his family had moved to Texas in 1845. He went into the cattle business in 1856 with his step-brother. Their job was to look after some 400 cattle from a nearby ranch. Their pay was every fourth calf which was born, and by 1860 they themselves owned 180 cattle. Like many young Texans, Goodnight fought in the Civil War when it broke out in 1861.

When the cattlemen returned to Texas after the war, they found that their farms and ranches were in a poor state and their cattle had run wild. When Goodnight and his step-brother rounded up their own herd, it had increased to some 5000 head of cattle. Here was a way to get rich! Sell the cattle and make a profit! Goodnight, together with many other Texans, began the trails to the North to sell his cattle to the growing and hungry cities. By the spring of 1866, Goodnight had 8000 head of cattle, ready to be driven north. He had heard, however, of the angry mobs and the cattle rustlers who attacked the cattle drovers on their way to Sedalia. He had the idea that there might be a good market in New Mexico, where 7000 Navaho Indians were held captive near Fort Sumner (see map on page 63). He and Oliver Loving, an experienced cattle driver, decided to try to reach Fort Sumner. In 1860 Loving had driven a herd as far west as Denver to sell beef to feed the

Colorado gold miners. He was the ideal partner for such a venture.

Goodnight and Loving gathered together 2000 cattle and eighteen cowboys. Goodnight also designed what is said to be the first chuck wagon (see page 69) to be pulled by ten oxen. Goodnight and Loving knew that there would be problems with this route. They could be attacked by Comanche Indians, so they had to take a route which went south first, over the Texas plains. You can see the route which they took on the map on page 63. One big problem was that on this route they would have to be without water for a very long time. It was this lack of water which nearly ruined their drive. Cows, steers, bulls and men all suffered. Many animals died of thirst and exhaustion, and the men were growing weary and restless. Suddenly, the cattle scented water! It was the Pecos River, some 20 kilometres away. The animals stampeded, very weakly, to the river. Goodnight and Loving rested the herd there. The animals fattened on the grassy banks and enjoyed the waters of the river.

At the end of the trail they found that, despite all the problems, they had lost only 300 head, and they were able to drive the remaining 1700 to Fort Sumner to sell to the Government to feed the starving Navaho. Most important of all, they made a huge profit on the drive.

Oliver Loving drove the rest of the herd, which they had not sold, north to Denver, Colorado, where he was able to sell them for good profit to John Iliff, whom we shall meet again later. Goodnight was ready to start again, so he rode east from Fort Sumner to buy another herd to trail west again. He also had about $12,000 in his pack-saddles.

Despite the success of Goodnight and Loving, problems like Indian attacks were never solved on this trail. It was, after all, on the trails further east that a way was found to lessen the dangers facing cattlemen.

Joseph McCoy and Abilene

The long drive northwards with the Texas-reared Longhorns fast became big business in the years after the Civil War. Profits could be enormous, and the Longhorns were ideal animals. They were hardy enough to stand up to the drive, and, very importantly, they provided a lot of meat. As long as the industrial cities of the North were growing and willing to pay handsomely for the meat which they needed, cattlemen would drive their herds up from Texas.

What were they to do, though, about the hostility of the people of Kansas and Missouri? Charles Goodnight and Oliver Loving had taken a trail much further west, but they were making for Colorado. Others, wanting to sell to the buyers from the East, had turned their trail east, along the Missouri-Arkansas boundary, heading for St Louis, or some other point east of Sedalia. This route, though, provided very poor grazing for their herds. How could the cattlemen use the best trails *and* avoid the armed mobs?

Joseph McCoy, a cattle dealer from Illinois found the ideal solution.

'The plan was to establish at some accessible point a depot or market to which a Texan drover could bring his stock unmolested, and there, failing to find a buyer, he could go upon the public highways to any market in the country he wished. In short, it was to establish a market whereat the Southern drover and the Northern buyer would meet upon equal footing, and both be undisturbed by mobs or swindling thieves.'

Here, McCoy decided, he would build a town specially for the purpose of cattle dealing. The place which he chose was Abilene, on the Kansas-Pacific railroad. From there, stock could be taken to Chicago by railroad. Why did he choose Abilene? It was, as yet, undeveloped. It had all the grass and water which would be needed when all those thousands of cattle would be gathered there, waiting to be sold. It was also, as McCoy himself said, 'the farthest point east at which a good depot for the cattle business could have been made'.

McCoy worked furiously to make Abilene into the first cow-town – and he had a great deal to do. He described Abilene in 1867 as 'a very small, dead place, consisting of about one dozen log huts, low, small, rude affairs, four fifths of which were covered with dirt for roofing', McCoy had timber sent to Abilene and built offices and cattle-pens. He even built a hotel, called the Drover's Cottage! In 1867 drovers took about 36,000 cattle along the Chisholm Trail from Fort Worth to Abilene. By 1870 the number of cattle had grown to over 300,000, and Abilene had three more hotels and ten saloons, or bars. Between 1867 and 1881, nearly one and a half million head of cattle passed through Abilene, being sent on to towns like Kansas. McCoy had been right about the need for a cattle town – and this was only the beginning.

Loading cattle into Kansas stock cars in Wichita 1874

Ranching on the Great Plains

The growth of Abilene as a cow-town marked the start of the spread of the cattle kingdom from Texas to the Plains. Cattle from Abilene began to cover the Great Plains and the cattle which were not sold were put out to grass on the Plains. New cattle towns were built as the railroad went further west – Dodge City, Wichita, Ellsworth. New trails were blazed to connect with the railroad at these points. Dodge City had enormous success as a cow-town between 1875 and 1885. About one quarter of a million head of cattle were driven to Dodge City from Texas and then taken by rail to be slaughtered in Chicago or Kansas City.

The success of the long drives and the cow-towns did not last. The last big drives to the North were in 1886, and by 1895 there were no more. It was not, however, the end of the cattle business. Instead, cattle ranching began to spread northwards, from Texas onto the Great Plains themselves. Why did this happen, when Abilene was such a success?

The railroads across the Plains had been a route to riches for the cattlemen. They also, however, brought people who began to settle on and to farm the Plains. The settlers' farms began to block the trails, so cattlemen were forced to take routes westwards.

The Indians, too, made life difficult for the drovers. In 1868 the US Government had granted land to the Indians, as you will see later (Chapter 7, pages 108–9). Now the Indians began to make the cowboys pay to drive the cattle across Indian land. The cattlemen began to think that it would be easier to raise the cattle on the Plains themselves. In 1870 Charles Goodnight bought a plot of land on the Arkansas River near Pueblo, Colorado, and used cattle driven up from Texas to stock his range there. Others followed his example. By 1880 cattle ranches had been set up in six territories in the northern Plains, all stocked with Texas Longhorns. The figures below show us just how far cattle ranching spread in the northern Plains in the years between 1860 and 1880.

Figures for the cattle industry on the northern Plains

State/Territory	Cattle, 1860	Cattle, 1880
Kansas	93 455	1 533 133
Nebraska	37 197	1 113 247
Colorado	none	791 492
Wyoming	none	521 213
Montana	none	428 279
Dakota	none	140 815

(From the Tenth Census of the US, 1880)

John Iliff

John Iliff is a good example of a man who made a success of ranching on the northern Plains.

Iliff, born in 1831, was the son of an Ohio farmer. He left home when he was twenty-five for the pioneer life of the West. He set up as a trader in Kansas, selling food and equipment to those on the California and Oregon Trails. He moved out to Colorado in 1859, after gold had been discovered near Pike's Peak, to trade with the miners. He soon began to graze a few cattle, and before long realised that he could make more money as a cattle rancher than as a trader. Iliff's cleverest move was then to buy the herd which Oliver Loving brought to Colorado in 1866 (see page 64). This was far better than picking up the cattle which, foot-sore from the route west with the wagon trains, were left on the Plains. Many other traders followed Iliff's example.

Iliff realised that he would have to make the most of every opportunity. The Union Pacific Railroad construction gangs, who had set up camp near Cheyenne, needed meat. Iliff won a contract to supply them with beef at $6.90 per 100 pounds. When the railroad reached Cheyenne, Iliff was able to send his beef to the cities of the East. Slaughtered cattle were put in iced railroad cars and sent east to Chicago.

At the same time, in 1872, Iliff managed to win another contract, to supply beef to Red Cloud and over 7000 Sioux Indians who had been moved to an area of land near Fort Laramie. Iliff's business continued to prosper – a combination of luck and good business sense. He bought huge numbers of cattle from Texas, and began to experiment with breeding. He crossed his Longhorns with Durham and Hereford bulls brought from England. These produced more meat and more milk than the Longhorns, but were less hardy. This did not matter once the cattle were on the Plains ranches. They had no need to be as tough as the Longhorns which had survived the long drives so well.

The open range

The ranches on the Plains often covered hundreds of thousands of hectares. The cattle roamed freely over them to graze on the grass. Water supplies were important and ranchers competed fiercely to take over land near running streams. The ranchers dug deep wells if there were no streams. Rainfall was small, and each rancher needed a huge area to graze his cattle. No rancher, however, could afford to buy all the land over which his cattle roamed. The land was, in fact, not owned by anyone – it was unfenced, the 'open range'. Each rancher had his 'range rights' on the land. This included the right to reserve a stream or a water-hole for his cattle, together with the land which ran back to the next 'divide' which separated his watering place from the next.

Men like John Iliff realised that the best place to buy land was along the rivers. In this way they could then control much of the land behind the rivers. The cattle, however, wandered freely. They did not know where one man's rights or land ended and another's began. This was where the brandmark was important. The brandmark told the rancher which were his cattle, and it was the cowboy who had the task of rounding up, branding and looking after these herds of cattle on the open range.

In the early days of cattle ranching, when cattlemen had had to move with their herd, they, like the Plains Indians, had to adapt to the life of the Plains in dug-outs and make-shift shacks. Now that the cattle were raised on the Plains themselves, the rancher would build sturdy living-quarters for himself and his cowboys when they were not 'riding the range'. Men were, at last, beginning to settle on the Great Plains, and one of best known figures at this time, without which cattle ranching would have been impossible, was the cowboy.

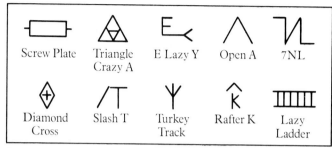

Brandmarks

SOURCE WORK: Cattle ranching on the northern Plains

SOURCE A

'His first care will be to select a location that has living or running water, as much timber and other shelter as possible, with a large tract of unsettled and untillable country surrounding it. It is important to choose such a location, that when he has purchased a reasonably sized tract of land he will own all the water and tillable land in the vicinity for miles around, otherwise he may have agricultural neighbours in such near proximity as to interfere with the free ranging and grazing of his stock.'
(J. G. McCoy, *Historic Sketches of the Cattle Trade of the West and Southwest*, Millett and Hudson 1874)

1 Why would a rancher need running water and timber?

2 It appears that the rancher wanted to get as far away as possible from farmers. Cattlemen and farmers used the land in different ways. Why, then, would cattlemen not want farmers as near neighbours?

SOURCE B

This is from a letter written by J. Wham, Indian Agent for Red Cloud's reservation, to the Indian Affairs Commissioner in Washington. It is dated 20 February, 1872.

'On taking charge of the Red Cloud Indians at Fort Laramie, I saw their allowance of beef was insufficient for their subsistence if kept at an Agency where they could not keep game. I asked, therefore, the Department of the Interior for authority to increase the ration when necessary. In the meantime the Indians were clamouring for more beef. And threatening to leave the Agency and go where they could get game if I could not increase the ration. There were then at the Post upwards of 7000 Indians.'
(*Records of the Red Cloud Agency*, Bureau of Indian Affairs, National Archives and Record Service, Washington DC)

3 Source B is describing how the Indian Agent tried to get more beef for the Sioux in Red Cloud's reservation. He was successful.
You read on page 66 how John Iliff won a contract to supply beef to Indians.
a) Are this and Source B about the same contract? Explain your answer.
b) Why was John Iliff a successful drover?

4 The figures on the opposite page sum up the great expansion of cattle rearing on the northern Plains. Use this chapter and any of the sources to help you to explain, in your own words, why this expansion took place.

Cowboys

Fact or fiction

'A cowboy's life is a dreary, dreary life,
Some say it's free from care;
Rounding up the cattle from morning till night
In the middle of the prairie so bare.' ©

'In without knocking': a painting by Charles M. Russell

What was it really like to be a cowboy? The cowboy in the song above doesn't seem to think much of it! The two pictures give very different impressions. One shows how Charles Russell, who worked on ranches between 1880 and 1892, saw the high-spirited cowboys at the end of a drive. The other is by Frederic Remington, who had briefly worked on a sheep ranch in Kansas, but gained most of his experience of the West from his travels there. This picture shows a cowboy on the trail looking wet and dejected. What was the cowboy's life really like?

A cowboy's life certainly meant long distances, hard work, dust and tiredness. It also seemed to attract restless young men who wanted adventure. Ross Santee (who was himself once a cowboy) published a book in 1926 called *Men and Horses*. In it he makes one of his characters explain his longing to be a cowboy:

'I always wanted to be a cow-puncher. When I was a little kid on the farm in East Texas I couldn't think of nothin' else. Most kids, I guess, is that-a-way, but they never could knock the idea out of me. . . . I stuck it out until I got to be about fifteen. Then I pulled out for good. I've never been home since.'

Many cowboys were ex-Confederate soldiers. Some were black ex-slaves from the southern states. Others, like the one in Ross Santee's book, were young men from farming lands, who wanted a life with more adventure than farming could offer.

The cowboy's job was to look after the herds of cattle on the range. He rode the range for most of the year rounding up cattle and branding them. He rode round the boundaries of the range to make sure that no-one took over these distant parts. This was called 'riding the line'. Then he had to drive the cattle to market. In the days of the long drives from Texas to railheads like Sedalia or Abilene, the cowboy spent most of his time on the trail. He lived and slept in the open. When ranching on the Plains began to take over from the long drives, the cowboy had a bunkhouse in which to sleep when he was not riding the line and driving the cattle to market. Was the job as attractive and romantic as the stories and the films make out? Or was it merely tiring and dirty?

Let us begin by having a look at the long drive.

'Riding a herd in the rain': a painting by Frederic Remington

The long drive: preparations

The cowboys rounded up the cattle in spring and sorted them out. Unmarked cattle were roped and branded if it was certain who owned them. There were often quarrels over unmarked animals!

The Longhorns were all called cows, whether they were cows, calves or steers. The general term 'beef' or 'beeves' was used for animals over four years old. The cowboys might drive their own boss's herd, or

Cowboys on the trail

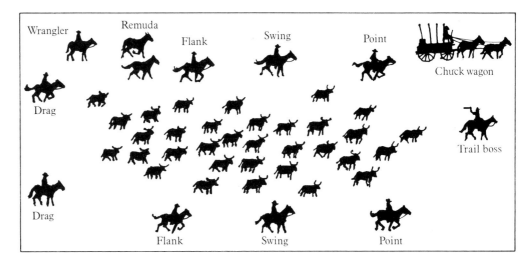

several herds, and the trail might be up to a mile long. This meant that the cowboys had to be well organised. Each one had to have a specific job, so that the cows did not wander away. Loss of animals meant loss of profit for the boss – and lower wages for the cowboys.

The diagram above shows how the cowboys were organised on the trail. The Trail Boss (sometimes called the 'ramrod') led the trail. His was an important job, and he might earn between $100 and $125 per month, which was good money. There were usually about ten other members of the outfit. The 'point' riders led the herd at the front of each flank, followed by the 'swing' men and line-riders (or flank-riders) at intervals along the main body of the herd. At the rear came the 'drag' or 'tail' drivers, who were usually young novices. Their job was to push along the lazy cows, riding the whole time in the dust kicked up by the herd. The spare horses, known as the 'remuda', were driven by the 'wrangler'. He was usually a young man learning the job of a cowboy. They were kept in a rope corral, or enclosure, when they stopped. The last member of the team was the cook. He was probably the most important member, but was often hired only because he could drive cattle and not because he could cook! He sometimes also had the job of burying the dead. The cook was in charge of the chuck-wagon. It was the chuck-wagon which held the cooking and eating utensils, as well as the cowboys' bedding rolls. The cook's importance is shown by the fact that he would earn more than the other men – about $50 per month compared with $35 per month.

Life on the trail

The herd had to be guarded all night as well as during the day. The photograph above shows the night guard. The night guard was difficult and tiring.

A restless cow could disturb all the others, and the cowboys had to have some sleep after the dust and the dangers of the long day's driving. Cowboys often sang to the herd to keep them calm:

'O say, little dogies, when you goin' to lay down
And quit this forever siftin' around?
My limbs are weary, my seat is sore;
O lay down dogies, like you've laid before.
Lay down little dogies, lay down.' ©

Those who were not on the night watch slept in the open, with only their oilskin slicker (rain-cape) to keep off the rain. Despite the discomfort, they would sleep soundly for as long as they were allowed to sleep, and this was often only four or five hours. They sometimes had to rub tobacco juice into their eyes to make them smart and keep themselves awake.

The cowboys moved the herd fast to begin with, and then slowed down to about 16 to 25 kilometres per day. This meant that the cows could graze as much as possible, and so be fat for the market.

There were dangers and problems at every turn. One of the worst dangers, and the dread of every cowboy's life, was the stampede. This was particularly likely during the first few days of the drive, when the cows were nervous and ready to bolt at anything. Sometimes old bulls were included in the herd to calm the young cows down. Anything could cause a stampede, from a flash of lightning to the neighing of a horse. All hands were called in to turn the stampeding herd in on itself in a circling mass until they stopped, exhausted. The cowboy on his horse, trying to keep up with a stampeding herd, could be tripped and trampled to death.

Another danger was being sucked under or caught in currents when crossing rivers. There were also scorpions and poisonous snakes, quicksands and, sometimes, hostile Indians when the trail crossed Indian land.

SOURCE WORK: Cowboys: their life and work

SOURCE A

The next extract was written by Theodore Roosevelt, who was President of the United States between 1901 and 1909. As a young man he lived the rough life of a cowboy for some time, and even raised a regiment of cowboys to fight in the war against Spain which broke out in 1898.

'During the early spring months before the round-up begins, the chief work is in hauling out mired [*stuck in bog or mud*] cows and steers. . . . As long as everything is frozen solid there is, of course, no danger from miring; but when the thaw comes along towards the beginning of March . . . the frost goes out of the soil, the ground round every little alkali-spring changes into a trembling quagmire, and deep holes of slimy, tenacious [*clinging*] mud form in the bottom of the gullies. The cattle, which have had to live on snow for three or four months, are very eager for water, and are weak and in poor condition. They rush heedlessly into any pool and stand there, drinking gallons of icy water and sinking steadily into the mud.'

(T. Roosevelt, *Ranch Life and the Hunting Trail*, The Century Co. 1896)

SOURCE B

Teddy 'Blue' Abbott had been a cowboy himself, and knew well what the long drive was like. This is an extract from a book which he wrote called *We Pointed Them North*.

'The poorest men always worked with the drags, because a good hand wouldn't stand for it. I have seen them come off the herd with the dust half an inch deep on their hats and thick as fur in their eyebrows and moustaches, and if they shook their head or you tapped their cheeks, it would fall off them in showers. The dust was the reason a good man wouldn't work back there, and if they hires out to a trail outfit and were put with the drags, they would go to the boss and ask for their time.'

(E. C. Abbott, *We Pointed Them North*, University of Oklahoma Press 1966)

SOURCE C

This extract comes from the diary of George Duffield, who drove a herd of 1000 Longhorns from Southern Texas to Iowa in 1866.

'May 8   Rain pouring down in torrents. Ran my horse into a ditch and got my knee badly sprained.

May 14   Brazoz River. Swam our cattle and horses and built raft and rafted out provisions and blankets and so on over. Swam river with rope and then hauled wagon over. Lost most of our kitchen furniture such as camp kettles, coffee pots, cups etc.

June 1   Stampede last night among 6 droves and a general mix up and loss of beeves. Hunt cattle again. Men all tired and want to leave.

June 2   Hard rain and wind storm. Beeves ran and I had to be on horseback all night. Awful night. Men still lost. Quit the beeves and go hunting men is the word – 4 p.m. Found our men with Indian guide and 195 beeves 14 miles from camp. Almost starved not having had a bite to eat for 60 hours. Go to camp about 12.00. Tired.

June 19   Arkansas River. 15 Indians came to herd and tried to take some beeves. Would not let them. Had a big Muss. One drew his knife and I my revolver. Made them leave but fear they have gone for others.'

1 Look at Sources A–C.
   What do these sources tell us about problems which cowboys had with:
   i) the weather?
   ii) difficult ground?
   iii) dust?
   iv) Indians?
   v) the cattle themselves?

2 The extract from J. G. McCoy's book (Source D on page 71) says that 'His life borders nearly upon that of an Indian'. What do you think he means by this?

SOURCE D

A photograph of a cowboy of the 1880s

3 Look back at page 62, where you will see a picture of a Mexican *vaquero*. His clothes are very similar to those of the cowboy in Source D (above). Did the American cowboys just copy the *vaqueros*, or was there some reason for wearing clothes like these? Explain your answer in as much detail as you can.

SOURCE E

'The life of the cowboy is one of considerable daily danger and excitement. It is hard and full of exposure, but is wild and free, and the young man who has long been a cowboy has but little taste for any other occupation. He lives hard, works hard, has but few comforts and fewer necessities. He has but little, if any, taste for reading. He enjoys a coarse practical joke or a smutty story; loves danger but hates labor of the common kind; never tires of riding. He would rather fight with pistols than pray; loves tobacco, liquor and women better than anything else. His life borders nearly upon that of an Indian.'
(J. E. McCoy, *Historic Sketches of the Cattle Trade of the West and Southwest*)

SOURCE F

Extracts from the Rules of the X. I. T. Ranch, 1888

No. 11 No employee of the Company is permitted to carry on or about his person or saddlebags any pistol, dagger, knuckles, bowie knife or any other similar instruments for the purposes of offense or defense.

No. 12 Card playing and gambling of every description is strictly forbidden on the ranch.

No. 15 Employees are strictly forbidden the use of vinous, malt, spiritous or intoxicating liquors during their time of service with the Company.
(J. Evetts Haley, *X. I. T. Ranch of Texas and the Early Days of the Llano Estacado*, University of Oklahoma Press 1953)

4 Read Sources E and F.
  a) What *differences* can you find between the way they show the cowboy's life?
  b) Does this mean that one source is wrong?

SOURCE G

'As I muse over my past life it occurs to me that possibly more has been written about the American cowboy, more has been said, more moving-pictures made of and about him, than any other character in American history. I am proud to have been one of those early day cowboys. He is the most romantic, most glamorised and most misunderstood figure ever to ride across the pages of our history.'
(Milt Hinkle, in *True West Magazine*, No. 47, October 1961, Western Publications Inc.)

5 Milt Hinkle is here writing about the way in which cowboys and their life have continued to fascinate people.
  a) Which aspects of a cowboy's life do you think would appeal most to
    i) Modern-day Americans?
    ii) Modern-day Europeans?
  b) Are these aspects similar to those which appealed to Ross Santee's young cowboy?

6 Look back at the sources which you have used in this section, and at any relevant parts of the chapter. Why do you think that Milt Hinkle says that the cowboy is 'romantic' and 'misunderstood'?

The end of the open range

The winter of 1886–7

If the Plains were to go on supporting vast numbers of cattle, they needed good grass, and for this they needed good weather. Even with good weather, however, the Plains grass would grow thin with so many cattle feeding on it. Many cattlemen realised that they might have to think about fencing their land to protect their own grazing areas from their neighbours' cattle.

By 1882 the profits from cattle ranching were beginning to go down. Fencing was expensive, and the more cattle which were sent to the Chicago stock yards, the lower the prices they fetched. There was just too much meat. When some ranchers realised this they began to sell their herds. This meant that prices went down even further.

The real death blow to the cattle boom, however, was out of the hands of any man. It was the weather. Beginning with the cold, blustery winter of 1885–6, it hit at stock and cattlemen alike. The summer of 1886 was so hot and dry that it withered the grass and dried up the streams. Ranchers panicked and many sold their herds, even at low prices. They were glad that they did. The winter of 1886–7 was the worst

'Waiting for the chinook; last of 5000?': Russell's painting of the 1886–7 winter, when hopes of the warm dry chinook wind were far away

in living memory. It became legendary for the depth of the snow, the storms and the temperatures which went as low as -68°C. Cattle could not reach the grass through the frozen snow. The worst blizzards which anyone could remember caused the cattle, usually so hardy, to die in their thousands. Russell's painting shows the way in which the hopes of many a cattleman died with the wasted flesh of his last Longhorn.

Even the good summer of 1887 did not help most ranchers. Some survived, and some drove their stock further westwards, to the grazing lands of Arizona and Eastern Oregon. Thousands went bankrupt. These tended to be the ranchers with smaller herds who had enough hay to feed around 200 head of cattle. They also had enough shelter around the ranchhouse to save the cattle from the worst of the weather. In the spring they were able to buy more, very cheaply.

The end of the open range

The days of the open range, though, were over. The cattle and the grass had to be balanced, and that meant fencing off the ranges, limiting the size of the herds and growing hay for winter fodder. The ranchers and the cowboys may not have wanted their old life-style to change, but they really did not have any choice if cattle ranching was to survive at all. There were, however, two major problems in fencing off land succesfully. The first was the need for fencing which was sturdy enough to keep one rancher's cattle in and another's out. The second, more importantly, was the need for water.

Two inventions played a big part in enabling land to be fenced. In 1874, Joseph Glidden, an Illinois farmer, produced a successful pattern of barbed wire. There had been dozens of attempts to make good barbed wire before Glidden's success, but none took off as his did. By the early 1880s, machines were producing huge quantities of Glidden's wire. In 1880 alone, about 36,600 tonnes were made and sold!

The farmers, as you will see in the next chapter, were the first to make use of barbed wire. They fenced off their holdings, and the cattlemen hated them for it. Fence-cutting wars broke out in places like Texas and Wyoming, where farmers' and cattlemen's demands on land met and clashed. In the end, though, the cattlemen realised that if they were to survive they would have to use barbed wire for themselves.

Without water, though, fenced-off land was no use. Not every rancher was able to enclose his land around a running stream. Not every stream provided enough water for a whole herd throughout the year.

An advertisement for Joseph Glidden's barbed wire, 1881

The problem was solved by the wind pump, which ranchers used to pump up water from underground. Some wind pumps were huge and fixed in place, like the one which you can see on page 87 of Chapter 5. There were also portable ones. This meant that supplies of water could be reached wherever the herds were pastured. Ranchers could now fence off their land even if there was no running water at all.

Once the stock was fenced in, the rancher could experiment with cross-breeding. He could keep count of his cattle without the round-ups and the branding of the open range. The cowboy was still there, but his job had changed. He now spent his time putting up and repairing fences, haymaking and feeding the stock. He moved the herds from pasture to pasture to allow grass to grow again, and rounded up stock in a much more limited area and in a way which was organised very differently from before. The day of the cowboy was over. The Great Plains were now no longer vast open spaces, roamed over by Longhorns, and settled by ranchers on huge open ranges. They were far from being the Great American Desert which men thought no-one would ever tame. The cowboys no longer lived a life, as they had done, like that of the Plains Indians, depending on horses and following the herds, and adapting their life to fit in with the Plains. Instead they became range-hands on fenced-in ranges with big pastures and carefully reared cattle. The day of the cowboy was over, but the day of the homesteader who farmed the Plains was coming.

SOURCE WORK: The end of the open range

SOURCE A

'I hate to see a wire fence
A-closin' up the range;
And all this fillin' in the trail
With people that is strange.
We fellers don't know how to plow
Nor reap the golden grain;
But to round up steers and
   brand the cows
To us was allus plain.' ©

(A cowboy song, in J. and A. Lomax, *Cowboy Songs*, Macmillan 1910)

SOURCE B

'When I saw a barbed wire machine at work manufacturing it and was told that there were thousands of them at the same work, I went home and told the boys they might just as well put up their cutters and quit splitting rails and use barbed wire instead.'

(W. S. James, *Cowboy Life in Texas*, M. A. Donahue and Co. 1893)

SOURCE C

'The first thing that especially roused the indignation of the stockman was the terrible destruction to stock caused from being torn first on the wire, and the screw worm doing the rest – this was especially the case with horses. When the first fences were made, the cattle, never having had experience with it, would run full tilt right into it, and many of them got badly hurt.'

(W. S. James, *Cowboy Life in Texas*)

1 a) What different arguments against barbed wire can you find in the sources on this page?
  b) Do you think that cattlemen and cowboys would have had different reasons for opposing the use of barbed wire? If so, what were these different reasons?
  c) Why, then, did cattlemen eventually use barbed wire?

2 Was barbed wire the *only* cause of the end of the open range? Explain your answer.

5

THE HOMESTEADERS

A land unfit for cultivation

'It is almost wholly unfit for cultivation, and of course uninhabitable by a people depending upon agriculture for their subsistence [*living*] . . . the scarcity of wood and water . . . will prove an insuperable obstacle in the way of settling the country.'

This was how Edwin James saw the Great Plains. He was a member of an expedition across the Plains in 1819–1820. He went on to say:

'The whole of this region seems particularly adapted as a range for buffaloes, wild goats and other wild game; incalculable multitudes of which find ample pasturage and subsistence upon it [*are able to feed well upon it*].'

Big Elk, of the Ponca Indians, agreed with him:

'For although I am but a poor simple Indian, yet I know that this land will not suit your farmers; if I even thought your hearts bad enough to take the land, I would not fear it, as I know there is not wood enough on it for the use of whites.'

Both Edwin James and Big Elk quite clearly ruled out the possibility of the Great Plains ever being farmed. There was not enough water, not enough wood, and the soil would only grow the sort of grasses which would feed wild animals, buffalo and cattle. You have seen, in the last chapter, how the cattlemen and cowboys made good use of the rich grasses and built up large and profitable ranches. They adapted themselves and their way of life to the Great Plains. They did not try to change the land or what was growing there. It was the homesteaders who determinedly battled against tremendous odds to tame the Plains and turn them into rich farmland.

Why choose the Great Plains?

What drove the early homesteaders to try to settle and farm on the Great Plains? Earlier farmers, as you have learned, saw the Plains as a terrible barrier which had to be crossed in order to reach the fertile farmlands of Oregon and California: However, by the 1860s most of the land there had been settled and was being farmed. It was therefore very expensive to buy.

Emigrants moving into Loup Valley, Nebraska, in 1886

For ordinary men and women in search of land, adventure, and a new start in life, the Great Plains offered them their only chance.

Who were these men and women who were prepared to take the enormous risk of farming land which others had considered impossible to farm? Some of the people who came to the Great Plains were freed slaves from the southern states. Others were immigrants from Europe trying to get away from poverty, unemployment and, sometimes, religious persecution. By far the largest group, however, were Americans from the states east of the Mississippi River.

It was not only the homesteaders themselves who wanted to see the Great Plains farmed and settled. Other people and organisations tried to encourage men and women to risk life on the Plains.

The role of the Government

The US Government, as you read in Chapter 3, wanted Americans to settle on the Great Plains. To encourage them to do this, the Government tried to make sure of two things. They tried to make it easy for the new settlers to own the land on which they settled. They also tried to keep law and order on the

Great Plains so that the new settlers could farm in peace and would not be forced to move on. How successful were they?

All the land opened for settlement in the West was 'public domain'. This meant that it belonged to no one and could be settled by anyone. The Government decided to change this. They tried to make sure that as much land as possible had an owner. The land was surveyed and divided into areas (of 9.6 square kilometres), called townships. Sometimes a whole township would be bought by one person or organisation. Usually though, the townships were divided up into sections of one square mile (640 acres or 259 hectares) and families would buy a section each. Each section was sold, at first, for a dollar an acre. However, it soon became clear that many ordinary people could not afford to buy a section in a township. Land speculators were moving in. They bought up all the land they could at 640 dollars a section, and sold it at high prices to the few settlers who could afford to pay.

This was not at all what the Government had wanted. In order to try to stop this they passed the Homestead Act in 1862. Under this Act the settlers were able to claim a section absolutely free, provided they had lived on it and worked it for five years.

The Great Plains were far from the Government in Washington and from the older, well established states. However, the Government still had to make sure that they were properly run and that law was kept and order maintained. The Government therefore organised the newly settled lands into Federal Territories, and appointed a governor to each one. This governor had to run the territory in the way in which the Government wanted. However, when a territory had 5000 free adult males living there it could have some say in the way it was governed. Responsibility for law and order, for example, was shared. The Government appointed federal marshals to see that Federal laws, which applied to everyone all over America, were obeyed. County sheriffs and town marshals were appointed locally. They were there to see that local laws, which differed from territory to territory and from state to state, were obeyed. The US Government, however, still had overall control because they appointed the governor and some of the officials.

When a territory had as many as 60,000 people living there it could become a state. It could look after its own affairs and choose its own governor. It could join the union of states which made up the United States of America. In these ways the Government hoped to encourage sensible, orderly settlement of the Great Plains.

States of the USA with dates of their admission into the Union

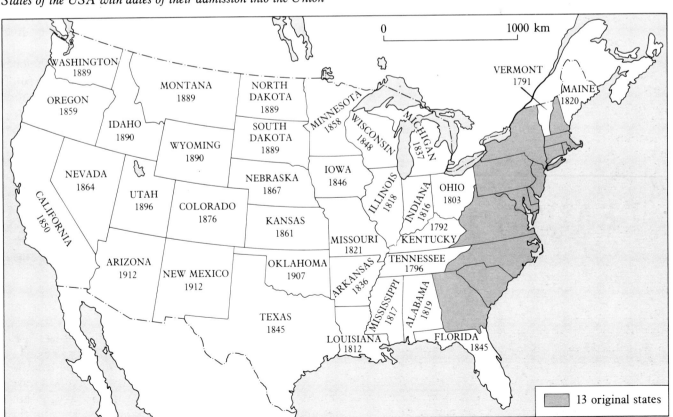

The role of the railroad companies

It was not only the Government which encouraged and made possible the settlement of the Great Plains. The US Government wanted a cross-continental railroad to be built from Washington in the East to California in the West. This would encourage trade and industry, and would also join together even more firmly the newly developing territories and states within America. To do this the Government needed the co-operation of the railroad companies.

It was not surprising that the railroad companies supported the Federal Government enthusiastically over this. They could see that it was a chance to make enormous profits. The Government could not give the railroad companies much money – but it could give them land. It gave the Union Pacific and Central Pacific railroad companies townships on either side of the railroad. The railroad companies could then sell this land. Money from the sale could be used to pay for more railroad building. The sale of land would, they hoped, attract more passengers and freight as more people would travel west and live and work out west. The railroad companies could build more track, and would be bound to prosper.

A railroad advertisement for land, 1875

'The modern ship of the plains' – travelling on an emigrant train in 1886. This drawing by R. F. Zogbaum first appeared in the magazine Harpers Weekly

The railroad companies began a massive advertising campaign not only in America but in the whole of northern Europe. Pamphlets and posters flooded Sweden, Norway, Denmark, Holland, Germany, France and England. Thousands of men and women were attracted by the promise of cheap land. They crossed the Atlantic, determined to make a good life for themselves and their families on the Great Plains. In Nebraska the Nebraska Immigration Association was founded, promising 'Land for the Landless' and 'Homes for the Homeless'. Dakota Territory voted 3000 dollars to help pay for the setting up of a Bureau of Immigration to attract settlers from abroad.

The Civil War

Thousands of people were persuaded to tackle the life of the homesteader as an indirect result of government action. A fierce and bitter Civil War had been fought in America between 1861 and 1865. On the one side were the slave-owning southern states, the Confederate states. They were fighting for the right to manage their own affairs and to opt out of the Union of states if they wished. On the other side were the industrial northern states, generally opposed to slavery, and determined that all the states within America should hold fast together in one Union. The northern states won. Thousands of former negro slaves fled the southern states to find a better life on the Great Plains. With them went hundreds of ex-soldiers from both Confederate and Union armies.

In the space of less than thirty years thousands of families moved on to the Great Plains. They came not only from the eastern and southern states of America, but also from the different countries of Europe. Most were farmers, but some were speculators, shopkeepers, administrators and school teachers. Despite their differences, all would have agreed that life on the Great Plains offered them a future which they would not otherwise have had.

SOURCE WORK: Travelling west

SOURCE A

A comment made in 1860 by a man who had often travelled over the Plains:

'You look on, on, on, out into space, out almost beyond time itself. You see nothing but the rise and swell of land and grass, and then more grass – the monotonous, endless prairie! A stranger travelling on the prairie would get his hopes up, expecting to see something different on making the next rise. To him the disappointment and monotony were terrible. "He's got loneliness", we would say of such a man.'

SOURCE B

As a boy, Hamlin Garland was taken to Iowa by his parents. He remembers:

'Each mile took us farther and farther into the unsettled prairie until in the afternoon of the second day, we came to a meadow so wide that its western rim touched the sky without revealing a sign of man's habitation other than the road in which we travelled. The plain was covered with grass as tall as ripe wheat and when my father stopped his team [*of horses, pulling the wagon*] and came back to us and said, "Well, children, here we are on The Big Prairie", we looked around us with awe.'

(Hamlin Garland, *A Son of the Middle Border*, Macmillan 1917)

1 Sources A and B describe the feelings which two people had about the Plains.
  a) How do Sources A and B help you to understand why people at first said that the Great Plains would never be settled?
  b) The Garland family would have understood the feelings of the stranger who had 'got loneliness' (Source A). Why did they stay and settle on the prairies if they, too, had felt like this at the start?

SOURCE C

This is the view of Percy Ebbutt, an Englishman who arrived in Kansas in 1870.

'You must make up your mind to rough it. You must cultivate the habit of sleeping in any kind of surroundings, on a board and without a pillow, indoors or out. I have been to sleep on horseback before now.

You must be prepared to cook your own dinner, darn your own socks if you wear them, and think yourself fortunate if you are not reduced to the position of a man I knew, who lay in bed while his wife mended his only pair of trousers. Learn to ride as soon as you possibly can; a man or boy who cannot ride is, in a new country, about as valuable as a clerk who cannot write in a city office.'

(Percy Ebbutt, *Emigrant Life in Kansas*, Swan-Sonnerschein 1882)

SOURCE D

An anti-slavery farmer who arrived in Kansas in 1860 wrote:

'We wanted to be in a free state, but I reckon there ain't no freedom here except to die of thirst.'

2 Explain carefully whether you agree or disagree with these statements:
  a) Percy Ebbutt was exaggerating the difficulties of life on the Plains in order to prevent people going there to settle.
  b) The anti-slavery farmer was clearly lazy as he hadn't even bothered to look for water and so he would be unlikely to make a success of living on the plains.

3 Look carefully at the poster opposite and read Sources C and D again. These sources all tell us something about the lands in Iowa, Nebraska and Kansas.
  a) Which source would have been the most useful, *then*, to a family thinking of moving west?
  b) Which source would be the most useful, *now*, to an historian trying to find out about the settlement of the West?

Getting started

Daniel Freeman was the very first homesteader to be registered under the Homestead Act as a land owner. On 30 January 1868 the government received the final registration payment of six dollars from him, and that meant that the land he had been farming was legally his. We know from the terms of the Act that he must have farmed or occupied the land for five years before asking to have his claim granted and the land made over to him legally.

We don't know whether or not Daniel Freeman was an honest man. There were many people who did all they could to get round the terms of the Homestead Act in order to get more land than that to which they were entitled. Many also tried to buy the land more cheaply, or to obtain land with less fuss and bother than the terms of the Act laid down. This meant that people who had no intention of farming tried to buy all the land they could, so that they could resell it to the homesteaders at high prices. Speculation like this, and the fact that the best land in townships was usually reserved for government buildings and state schools, meant that many genuine homesteaders either had to buy land or make do with land of poor quality.

Where shall we live?

In the early days of settlement on the Great Plains, whole families travelled west together. With the coming of the railroads, the men in the family would go west ahead of the women and children, and would only send for them when everything was ready. However, once a claim was staked and registered, all families faced the same problem: how to build a house. In this, as in everything else, the homesteaders were entirely dependent upon themselves.

They were dependent upon their own skill and courage in taking what they could from the Great Plains.

Obviously the homesteaders had to build with the raw materials which they had on their own claim. Most settlers lived far from the woods on the fringes of the Great Plains. They lived way out on the open plain, with no tree to be seen, and only the endlessly waving grass for miles and miles and miles. Houses could not be built from grass, but what else was there? There was the solid earth – and this is what the homesteaders used. First by hand, and later with specially built ploughs, blocks of earth called sods were cut and used as building bricks. This is what earned the homesteaders the nickname 'sod-busters'.

Sod houses had to be solid and strong. They had to withstand gales and storms, drought and blistering heat, grasshoppers and prairie fires. They also had to house men, women and children and keep them warm enough and well enough so that they could work hard enough to make a living from the bare earth outside.

It took about an acre (0.4 hectares) of land to provide enough sods to build an average sod house on the Great Plains. Once the grass sods were cut, they were used as bricks to build the walls, which were sometimes as much as a metre thick. Spaces were left for the windows and doors. The whole house would be roofed with long grass, more sods, or whatever was handy. It would then be plastered down and made more or less watertight with masses of clay-like mud which baked hard in the wind and the sun. Sod houses, properly built, were, as one proud owner stated: 'Mighty comfortable places to go in cold weather, and it doesn't take much fire to keep them warm'.

This was just as well. The homesteaders had no alternative!

The sod house of J. C. Cram and his family in Loup County, Nebraska, in 1886

SOURCE WORK: The Homestead Act

SOURCE A

This is an extract from *An Act to Secure Homesteads to Actual Settlers on the Public Domain, May 20th, 1862.*

'Any person who is the head of a family, or who has arrived at the age of twenty-one years,
and is a citizen of the United States, or who shall have filed his declaration of intention to become such
and who has never borne arms against the United States Government
or given aid and comfort to its enemies,
shall, from and after the first January eighteen hundred and sixty-three, be entitled to enter one quarter section or a less quantity of unappropriated public lands . . . after the land shall have been surveyed . . .

The person applying for the benefit of this act shall, upon application to the register of the land office in which he or she is about to make such entry, make affidavit [*swear*] . . . that such application is made for his or her exclusive use and benefit,
and that the said entry is made for the purpose of actual settlement and cultivation, and not either directly or indirectly for the use or benefit of any other person or persons whomsoever.

No certificate shall be given or patent issued therefor until the expiration of five years from the date of such entry;
and if, at the expiration of such time . . . the person making such entry, or . . . his widow . . . or heirs, shall prove by two credible [*truthful*] witnesses that he, she, or they have resided upon or cultivated the same for . . . five years . . .
and that he has borne true allegiance to the Government of the United States; then, in such case, he, she, or they, if at that time a citizen of the United States, shall be entitled to a patent (stating that they own the land). . . .

If, at any time after the filing of the affidavit . . . and before the expiration of the five years aforesaid, it shall be proven, after due notice to the settler,
to the satisfaction of the register of the land office,
that the person having filed such affidavit shall have actually changed his or her residence, or abandoned the said land for more than six months at any time, then and in that event the land so entered shall revert to the government . . .'

(W. Miller, *Readings in American Values*, Prentice Hall 1964)

1 a) Why was the Homestead Act necessary?
  b) Would a homesteader find it easier or more difficult to get land once the Homestead Act had been passed?

2 The Homestead Act made it clear what a homesteader had to do, and what he had not to do, in order to have his claim to land upheld. If the four homesteaders listed below all applied, five years after staking their claim, to be allowed to own the land which they claimed under the terms of the Act, would an official of a state land office have allowed this?
  Remember to explain your answer by quoting the exact part of the Act which has helped you to make up your mind.
  i) Peter Harden, who let a friend farm his land for three years whilst he farmed land in another section.
  ii) Thomas Dawson, who brought two people with him to swear that he had lived on and had farmed his land claim for five years.
  iii) Janet Webster, whose dead husband had staked a claim to the land on which she and her children had lived and worked for five years.
  iv) Matthew Jones, who went home to Liverpool in England to visit his family for a year after staking his claim to land.

3 What does the Homestead Act tell us about the way in which the US Government wanted the West settled?

'A woman's work is never done'

It was an achievement to build a house from sods of earth for yourself and your family, and to earn the nickname 'sod-buster'. It was an even greater achievement to live in a sod house successfully: so to manage day-to-day living that your family was warm, fed, clothed, clean and healthy. This, inevitably, was women's work.

The women who had travelled from the southern and eastern states of America, and those who had come from Europe, were faced with the same enormous problem. How were they to cope? They had learned to care for their families under very different conditions from those which they found on the Great Plains. Here on the Plains nothing was familiar. There was nobody to turn to, only other families with the same problems and difficulties as themselves. The women had to learn to do what they could with what they had. They had to learn quickly. Their own lives and the lives of their husbands and children depended upon their ability to adapt and invent.

Fuel and food

Every homesteader needed fuel. Without fuel the homesteader family would be cold, hungry and dirty. Since there were hardly any trees on the Plains, there was no wood to burn. The women in the great wagon trains which rolled westwards earlier in the century had discovered that dried buffalo dung burned well. The sod-buster's wife did the same. She collected barrow-loads of dried cow dung and buffalo dung (cow chips) and had fuel in plenty.

Cow chips would burn, but they burned very quickly. Stoves therefore had to be stoked up very frequently, particularly when there was cooking to be done. A boy described watching his mother bake:

'Stoke the stove, get out the flour sack, stoke the stove, wash your hands, mix the dough, stoke the stove, wash your hands, cut out the biscuits with the top of the baking powder can, stoke the stove, wash your hands, put the pan of biscuits in the oven, keep on stoking the stove until the biscuits are done.'

Meals were often monotonous and very boring. One schoolteacher, Mollie Sanford, living with a family of sod-busters, wrote:

'For breakfast we had corn bread, salt pork and black coffee. For dinner, greens, wild ones at that, boiled pork and cold corn bread washed down with 'beverage'. The 'beverage' was put upon the table in a wooden pail and dished out in tin cups. When asked if I would have some . . . I said "yes", thinking it perhaps was cider, but found out it was vinegar and brown sugar and warm creek water.'

Dirt and disease

Feeding a family was only part of what a woman had to do. Thomas Banning described how his mother kept the family clean:

'I have often wondered how my mother stood it with such a family of children and no one to help her but my oldest sister . . . We used soft soap that my mother made by leaching water slowly through a barrel of wood ash to get the alkali and potash, and then boiling this in a kettle with the scraps of fats she saved.'

People and clothes had to be kept clean, and so did houses. Most sod houses had an earth floor and sod walls which were sometimes plastered with mud and clay. Spiders, fleas and all kinds of insects lived in the walls and roofs. Even with modern detergents and vacuum cleaners it would have been impossible to keep such a house really clean. The sod-buster's wife had an uncertain water supply, little soap, rags, and brushes made from twigs. She fought an unending battle against dirt and disease.

In a country with few doctors, disease had to be prevented. This, too, was the job of the women, even if they were doctor's wives: 'My wife became unhappy for the first time when she saw bed bugs racing up the walls,' wrote Dr C. G. Barns in 1878. 'My wife had a good thick whitewash made, and plastered on the walls and got rid of the bugs.'

All the women had well-tried remedies for illness which they adapted to Plains life. These were the most common cures they used:

For a wound: apply turpentine or a red-hot ember from the fire.
For a cut: wrap it around with a cobweb.
For sick children: put a mustard poultice on their chests and onion poultices on their feet.
To cure a fever: wrap the sufferer's head in a cold cloth; wrap his feet in cabbage leaves and force him to swallow a mixture of rhubarb, cold tea and soda.
For snakebites: apply warm manure.
For earache: apply warm urine.
To cure measles: eat a well roasted mouse.

Pregnancy and childbirth

When women gave birth on the Great Plains there were no maternity hospitals and community midwives to help them. Charlie O'Kieffe tells us:

'According to what I've been told Mother herded cattle all day long in the broiling sun. The next morning around 2.00 am I was born. No doctor, no nurse, no midwife, just Mother and God; and 2 days later she was up and doing her regular housework.'

His mother may have felt differently! 'I do think a pregnant woman has a hard time of it,' wrote Susan Magoffin, not long after moving into her first home,

'Some sickness all the time, heart-burn, headache, cramp etc., after all this thing of marrying is not what it is cracked up to be.'

Teachers and teaching

Not all the women who travelled onto the Great Plains were married. In 1859 the *Lynne County* (Kansas) *Herald* printed an advertisement for: 'One hundred school marms, who will pledge themselves not to get married within three years.'

Schoolteachers were needed to teach the children living on the Great Plains and in the growing townships. The pay was usually low, and most teachers lived with the families of the children they taught. The 'schoolmarm' did not have to struggle in the same way as the homesteader's wife, but she had to struggle against prejudice and ignorance, and she had to work hard in appalling conditions.

'When she asked each child to bring his own drinking cup, a delegation of school directors appeared demanding to know the reason for such nonsense. She won the argument and proceeded to other matters. "There was not the slightest sign of a toilet. When I told the directors that I could not

teach if they did not build one, one of them remarked, 'Now you see what comes of hiring someone from the Outside. Never had any trouble before, plenty of trees to get behind'."'

Some 'schoolmarms' were tough in a different way. A man living on the southern edge of the Plains described his town's school teacher as an:

'Irish woman who had the strength of a strong man and the typical fighting spirit of her race. She kept a quart of whiskey and a leather quirt [*strap*] in her desk. The whiskey was strictly for her own use, the quirt for use on the kids.'

The woman 'schoolmarm', by insisting on certain standards of behaviour and speech, did a great deal to make the West a more civilised place. One old miner noticed the immediate change which came about when a school teacher came to set up school in his mining town. He wrote to a newspaper: 'So far as the improvement of society is concerned, one true, pure woman is worth a volume of sermons.'

This old miner would not have approved of all the women who went west. Some (as you will see later) could drink, swear and shoot as well as the men; others became prostitutes in the wild frontier towns. However, most women who went west were tireless, hardworking and dedicated. They were determined to do what they could with what little they had and to make life as good as possible for their families and for those for whom they were responsible.

Perhaps women did more to bring law and order to the West than the sheriffs and marshals you will read about in Chapter 6.

A 'schoolmarm' surrounded by her pupils, Nebraska, 1889

SOURCE WORK: Women settle the Great Plains

SOURCE A

A Prairie wife describes conditions:

'Sometimes the water would drip on the stove while I was cooking, and I would have to keep tight lids on the skillets to prevent mud from falling into the food. With my dress pinned up, and rubbers on my feet, I waded around until the clouds rolled by.'

(*The Nebraska Soddy* in *Nebraska History* (*Vol. 48*), Nebraska State Historical Society 1967)

SOURCE B

From the diary of a Nebraskan school teacher, Mollie Sanford:

'At this place I slept upon the floor, and festive bedbugs held high carnival over my weary frame [*body*] the night through.'

(M. Sanford, *Journal of Mollie D. Sanford 1857–66*, University of Nebraska Press 1959)

SOURCE C

A New England woman, writing from Kansas in 1855:

'We have but one room in which we all eat, drink and sleep, and that is not as large as your kitchen, and has got four chests, two trunks, a cook stove, an apology for a table, half a dozen bags, three or four stools, etc.'

(*New England Emigrant Aid Company Parties of 1855*, Kansas Historical Quarterly XV, 1947)

1 The women who wrote these three sources all lived in sod houses.
   a) What problems caused by living in these house does each source describe?
   b) What other problems were faced by people who had to live in sod houses?
   c) Life in a sod house was clearly not easy. Why, then, did the homesteaders live in them?

SOURCE D

'A warrior and a small band visited a tent camp, and seeing bright colored quilts and shiny utensils all about and no one near but a few "white squaws", he decided to help himself. One of the "white squaws", however, began defending her possessions with a heavy tent pole. "She laid it about, right and left, over heads, shoulders, and backs until she put them to flight." Next day the warrior returned, apologised for his conduct, and offered the woman's husband five hundred dollars for her. He was quite disappointed to learn she was not for sale.'

(Dee Brown, *The Gentle Tamers*, Putnam 1958)

SOURCE E

'. . . the Cheyenne warriors came upon Mrs Timothy Kine, a young mother who had taken her new baby to visit neighbors, Susan Alderdice and her four children. The two women saw the Indians approaching across the prairie. Mrs Kine plunged into the creek, at a point where she was hidden by some brush overhanging the bank, and held her baby high to keep it from drowning. But Mrs Alderdice, paralyzed with fear, collapsed in a faint, surrounded by her four quaking children. The Cheyennes shot the three oldest boys, killing two of them. They then galloped off with Mrs Alderdice and her youngest child. The baby cried so lustily that the Indians became enraged, choked it to death and left the body beside the trail. The gravely wounded mother later died.'

(H. Horn, *The Pioneers*)

2 Read these two sources carefully.
   a) What do they tell us about the attitudes of Indians towards white settlers?
   b) What do they tell us about the attitudes of white people toward the Indians?
   c) Look back at Chapter 2, and at the section 'The beliefs of the Plains Indians'. You will remember that Indians believed in the holiness of all living things. Do you, therefore, find it surprising that Indians attacked the homesteaders?

SOURCE F

'It was not wholly the fault of the sod house that contagious [*caught by touch*] diseases were common. The common drinking cup, the open dug well, the outdoor toilet (or no toilet at all) shared the blame with the lack of ventilation and crowded quarters of the sod house.

The floor of a dug out, or sod house, was commonly of clay dirt. It was not possible to scrub or disinfect it of the millions of germs that found a breeding place in the dirt trodden underfoot. The "no spitting" fad had not taken root . . . No wonder the mortality [*death rate*] by diphtheria was so great among children.

While those houses, as a rule, were warm in winter and fairly cool in summer for the human occupants, they favoured fleas and bed bugs by the million. Added to the lowering of vitality by lack of a balanced ration of food, lack of clothing, and changes of temperature, the wonder is not so much that disease and infection took a heavy toll, as the wonder that so many survived, to spend their later lives in modern houses.'

(C. G. Barns, *The Sod House*, University of Nebraska Press 1970)

3 In 1878, Dr C. G. Barns was a young doctor. He wrote, as you have seen, about his wife being upset because she saw bed bugs racing up the walls of their house (page 80).
   a) Why do you suppose Dr Barns himself was not upset by the sight of those bedbugs?
   b) What does Dr Barns suggest as being the main causes of contagious diseases in a sod house?
   c) By 1880 public health systems, which had piped water, earthenware (clay) pipes for sewerage and flushing lavatories, were in operation in many towns in the eastern states of America and in England.
      Why did the homesteaders go on using the remedies which you read about on page 80, instead of building lavatories and a proper sewerage system?

SOURCE G

'The chief figure of the American West . . . is not the long haired, fringed legging man riding a rawboned pony, but the gaunt and sad-faced woman sitting on the front seat of the wagon, following her lord wherever he might lead, her face hidden in the same ragged sunbonnet which had crossed the Appalachians and the Missouri long before. That was America, my brethren! There was the seed of America's wealth.'

(Emerson Hough, *The Passing of the Frontier*, 1921)

4 Read Source G carefully. Emerson Hough believed that women were very important in the history of the West. Use your knowledge of the part which women played in the settlement of the West to explain what he meant when he said that women were the 'seed of America's wealth'.

SOURCE H

'The Great Plains in the early period was strictly a man's country. . . . Men loved the Plains, or at least those that stayed there did. There was zest to the life, adventure in the air, freedom from restraint; men developed a hardihood which made them insensible to the hardships and lack of refinements. But what of the women? Most of the evidence, such as it is, reveals that the Plains repelled the women as they attracted the men. There was too much of the unknown, too few of the things they loved. If we could get at the truth we should doubtless find that many a family was stopped on the edge of timber by women who refused to go further. . . . Who can tell us how the Great Plains affected women, and why?'

(W. P. Webb, *The Great Plains*)

5 Now read Source H carefully.
   a) Emerson Hough and Walter Prescott Webb seem to disagree about whether men or women were the more important in the story of the Great Plains. Use what you know about the settlement of the Plains to explain whether you agree with the opinions of Emerson Hough or Walter Prescott Webb.
   b) How would you answer the question Walter Prescott Webb asks in the last line of the Source H?

Farming: the problems

Most of the people who set up as homesteaders in the West had had some experience of farming. However, they had learned to farm in the southern and eastern states of America or in Europe. There the soil and climate were very different from the soil and climate they found on the Great Plains. No one had farmed the Great Plains before. No one knew which crops to grow or how best to prepare the land. All the homesteaders could do was to try the methods which they knew had worked elsewhere.

Ploughing, sowing, harvesting and threshing

Before any crops could be grown, the ground had to be properly prepared so that the seed could be planted. Here was the farmer's first problem: the Great Plains had never before been ploughed. The grasses which grew there had roots which formed a dense tangled mat at least 10 cm thick. The cast iron ploughs which many farmers had brought with them buckled and broke under the strain, and had to be constantly repaired. The farmers could not afford to buy suitable machinery to do the job properly, whether that job was ploughing, sowing, harvesting or threshing. All too often, in any case, machinery was simply not available. Making the land productive was a slow and back-breaking job.

In Europe and the eastern and southern states of America lack of machinery was not really a problem because there were plenty of men and women willing to work on the farms. Here, in the West, there was a shortage of labour. Every farmer had to work his own land by himself to feed his own family.

An ox-drawn plough breaks the sod on a Kansas farm. This drawing appeared in Harper's Weekly *in May 1868*

Water

Lack of water was a desperate problem for all farmers on the Great Plains. The climate was extreme. In the winter temperature could fall to −40°C, and in terrible blizzards homesteaders could lose their way between their house and barn and die of exposure. In the summer temperatures could rise to above 80°C and stay there for weeks. The crops burned as they shrivelled in the parched ground. An average 38 cm of rain fell in a normal year on the Great Plains. This simply was not enough for normal agriculture. To make matters worse, it fell at the wrong time. Peak rainfall came in the summer, when the sun and hot winds dried up what moisture there was in the soil. Crops simply would not grow well – and sometimes they did not grow at all. Furthermore, not all years were 'normal'. A series of dreadful droughts hit Kansas and Nebraska, when no rain fell between January 1859 and November 1860. A regular supply of water was clearly essential.

The 'old' solutions – solutions which the farmers would have learned away from the Great Plains – would have been to irrigate or to dig wells. On the Plains irrigation was impossible because there were no rivers or lakes from which to dig drainage ditches. The only rivers were on the fringes of the Plains. To dig thousands of kilometres of ditches to carry an uncertain water supply across territory which was partly claimed and partly unclaimed, was clearly not sensible.

Many farmers did dig wells, but this was an expensive and uncertain business. In some places they had to dig shafts of up to 150m deep before they could get a reasonable supply of water from the ground. Homesteads with wells of their own rarely had enough water to irrigate the crops properly. A well could provide enough water for people and animals, but not enough to water the crops as well. Everyone went short as the precious water was shared between those who needed it. Sometimes water could simply not be found at all.

Land holdings

The size of a homesteader's holding was clearly important. It had to be large enough to provide enough to support himself and his family, and yet small enough for him to work by himself or with family help. An average holding was 160 acres (64.7 hectares). The Government decided upon 160 acres for administrative reasons – it was a quarter of a section. They also wanted to discourage people from setting up huge farms, like the great slave plantations of the South before the Civil War. However, with the poor rainfall and farming techniques learned hundreds of kilometres away from the Great Plains, the crop yield from 160 acres was just not enough to support the average homesteader and his family.

Crops

Farmers began by planting the crops they knew best. They planted corn (we call it maize or corn-on-the-cob), which always did well in the east where there was a lot of rain in the spring. They planted soft winter and spring wheats, which grew in the East where there was plenty of rain and no frost. Neither crop did well on the Plains, where there was low rainfall, scorching hot summers and extremely cold winters. In order to make farming a profitable business, any farmer has to grow crops which he can sell at a good price after harvest. It was the same for the sod-buster, except that he had first to find a crop which he could grow successfully.

Fencing

Homesteaders on the Plains, unlike the cattlemen, needed to fence in their land. They needed to do this so that they and their neighbours, no matter how far away they were, knew exactly which land was theirs. They also needed to stop cattle from straying onto their land and destroying the crops they were trying to grow. However, they had little timber with which to build fences, and hedging plants would not grow quickly enough, even if they survived.

Devastation : fire and grasshoppers

The homesteader had to cope with many hazards, but the most terrifying of these was fire. In the summer and autumn, when the prairie grasslands were bone dry, the merest spark could set off a fire which ran wild. Small fires could be dealt with efficiently by beating them out. Once a fire got a grip, however, there was nothing a homesteader could do but hide inside his sod house with his family while his crops were destroyed and the fire burnt itself out.

Devastation came from another source, and was every bit as deadly. Between 1874 and 1877 Rocky Mountain locusts (grasshoppers) swarmed through the Prairies devouring everything that came in their way. It seemed that there was nothing they wouldn't eat: crops and tree bark, leather boots and buckets, wooden door frames – even washing. The effects were terrible. Jennie Flint of Minnesota wrote to Governor Davis asking for help: 'We have no money nor nothing to sell to get any clothes with as the grasshoppers destroyed all of our crops'. The grasshoppers even managed to stop a Canadian Pacific train by swarming onto the rails and making them too slippery for the engine.

Clearly the homesteaders were determined to survive on the Great Plains and make some kind of a living from land so many others had rejected. However, if they were to do more than simply survive, they needed to find new ways of farming. New inventions, new discoveries or new techniques would be needed if the homesteaders were to succeed and prosper.

A maize field and sod house in Nebraska, 1880s. Look back at the picture of the sod house on page 78. Why do you think the sod houses were so different?

Farming: the solutions

The women adapted very quickly, as we have seen, to living in a sod house. The men took far longer to change their old ways of farming. This was partly because it took a long time for them to realise that the old methods were not suitable. It takes many months to realise that a crop is not growing properly, and several years to realise that one bad year is not an accident, but that all years will be bad. The 1870s were very bad years, and were for many homesteaders the final proof that they had to find new ways of overcoming their problems.

Machinery

Mass production of farm machinery meant that, gradually, mechanical reapers, binders and threshers became cheaper and farmers could afford to buy them. It wasn't only their cheapness which made them attractive. The early machines had to be returned to their makers if anything went wrong with them. The new machines had been re-designed not only to make them more efficient, but also so that they could be easily repaired. From the mid-1880s

An advertisement for McCormick's Patent Virginia Reaper, 1850

farm machinery helped the homesteader to cultivate more land without needing more men. A man with a sickle and flail could harvest 7.5 acres (3 hectares) of wheat in the same time that a man with a mechanical reaper could cover 100 acres (40.5 hectares).

Barbed wire

You have seen how the invention and production of barbed wire affected the cowboys and cattlemen. To the farmers on the Great Plains it was essential. It meant that they could quickly, efficiently and cheaply fence in their land. They could plant crops knowing that herds of cattle would not stray onto their land and trample and eat the growing plants. They could experiment with animal breeding, knowing that stray bulls would not mate with their stock. Without barbed wire the homesteaders could never have protected their land from the grazing herds of the cattlemen.

However, in trying to protect their own livelihood, the homesteaders destroyed that of other people. Barbed wire meant the end of the open range – and the cattlemen and cowboys were not going to give up easily, as we shall see later.

Wind pumps

Barbed wire may have made a homestead possible on the dry plains, but it did not make it profitable. The farmers could not always hold on to the homesteads they had staked out on the dry and arid Plains. They gave up because they could not find water – or because they could not find enough water. There was water below the surface soil, sometimes a long way below. The homesteaders needed some mechanical means of raising water to the surface. It would have to be cheap to build and cheap to run, and be able to produce water in a steady flow.

The wind pump was used by both cattlemen and railroads. It was soon quickly adapted to suit the needs of the farmer. First a high powered drill had to be used to drill a hole deep enough into the Plains to reach water. Sometimes this meant drilling several hundred metres. Then a wind pump was built to raise the water to the surface and to get it to where it was needed. It is hardly surprising that from the middle of the 1880s a wind pump dominated most of the homesteads on the Great Plains.

Railroads

Wind pumps and drills, barbed wire and mechanical reapers, threshers and binders were all essential to the prosperity of the farmer on the Great Plains.

A wind pump on a farm in Nebraska, 1888

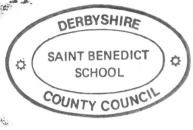

However, the Great Plains was not a place where people built barbed wire factories, or any other factory. How, then, was the farmer to benefit from these inventions? He benefited from them because of the railroads. We have seen how the railroads took the later homesteaders themselves out to their new lives on the Plains. They also transported quickly, cheaply and efficiently all that the homesteaders needed. The railroads brought ploughs and reapers, furniture and fabrics, steam traction engines and barbed wire to the homesteaders. The railroads brought all that was necessary for the homesteaders to farm well. They also made it possible for them to sell their crops in markets far from the Great Plains. The railroads were the homesteaders' only line of contact with the markets in the East where they sold their produce.

Legislation

The Government finally realised that 160 acres of land was not enough for successful farming on the Great Plains. In 1873 they passed the Timber and Culture Act, which allowed a homesteader to claim a further 160 acres provided that he promised to plant trees on half of it. This Act really did mean that the ordinary homesteader, who could not afford to buy land, was able to make a reasonable living.

Dry farming

Dry farming was a method of farming learned by the homesteaders on the Great Plains. It was a method which tried to keep the moisture in the soil by ploughing the soil every time it rained. The idea was that the moist soil would then be covered with a layer of fine dust, which would stop the moisture from evaporating. It might sound fantastic, but it actually worked. Water was conserved, and better crops could be grown.

Turkey Red

The soft wheats which the homesteaders had sown on the Plains were not suitable for such extremes of climate as were found there. In 1874 a group migrated from the Crimea area of Russia, bringing with them a new variety of wheat. This was Turkey Red. It was a hard wheat which could withstand frost and grow in the winter and spring when the chance of moisture was greatest. The mills, at first, were not suitable for grinding this new wheat. At first they were able to produce only a grey, sour powder. However, by 1881 a new method of milling hard wheat had been worked out. Growing Turkey Red wheat, using the dry farming method, was beginning to be very profitable indeed.

By itself, each of these inventions, discoveries and developments would not have ensured success for the homesteader on the Great Plains. Some were more important than others. Some were more important than others at different times and in different places and to different people. What is vital is that they all came together at the right time to enable the homesteaders, by 1890, to control the Great Plains. The homesteaders were no longer forced to change their lives to adapt to the Plains. They were able to force the Plains to become rich, fertile farmlands beyond the wildest imaginings of the early pioneers.

SOURCE WORK: Survival or prosperity?

SOURCE A

Howard Ruede's search for water.

'. . . using a borrowed three-piece auger [*hand drill*] and with Bub to help, Howard drilled a test hole two inches in diameter and 23 feet deep. There the brothers struck shale.

Not a drop of water seeped into the hole, but Howard was undismayed. He felt so confident of his luck, in fact, that he began to dig the well with a shovel. . . . [On 13 December] at a depth of 25 feet he ran into the same plate of shale which had stopped his auger. "There are men in this neighborhood who have dug 4 and 5 wells, and still have no water" he wrote.

Reverting to the auger, he and his brother bored two more holes – both dry. Next, his father caused a brief flurry of excitement with a hole he had dug, but hope quickly fizzled . . . "I ran a sunflower stalk down," Howard reported . . . "and the auger was only four feet deep with six inches of water in it. The misery of the thing is that it is not on my claim." The men tried another spot – this one back on their own property – and on March 24, 1878, in gravel a mere eight feet from the surface, they met success. Water gushed up at last – after five months of searching.'

(H. Horn, *The Pioneers*)

SOURCE B

Stuart Henry remembers the effect of the 1874 drought in Kansas.

'Hollow-eyed, fagged out, the fair sex came to care little how they looked, what they wore. . . . Men swore, and played poker no more. Fathers dreaded to face their children, who grew raggeder. As for their dirtiness, who, you might ask, hardly dared spare water to wash them? Husbands hated to go home to meals, for they must meet the appeal of their wives to climb on wagons and strike out for back home.'

(A. Nevins and H. Commager, *A History of a Free People*)

1 Read Sources A and B carefully.
   a) Explain whether the following conclusions could be correctly made after reading these sources:
      i) Howard Ruede must have been a bad farmer because it took him five months to find water which was only eight feet below the surface.
      ii) Women wanted to leave the Plains during the drought because there was no water in which to wash their children.
      iii) The homesteaders were stupid to settle on the Plains where there was no water.
   b) By 1890 the problem of lack of water on the Great Plains had almost been solved. How had this happened?

SOURCE C

An advertisement for Haish's improved 'S' barb steel fence wire

SOURCE D

'The transcontinental railroads immensely speeded up the economic and social development of the nation. . . . The region that benefited immediately was the Great Plains . . . the pioneers there were assured access to the wood and fuel necessary for existence, and guaranteed an outlet for their produce. It was only the coming of the railroads which meant that the conquest of the last unsettled frontier could begin.'

(Adapted from R. A. Billington, *Westward Expansion*, Macmillan 1967)

2 Look carefully at Source C.
The manufacturers of Haish's Improved S Barb Steel Fence Wire are clearly in no doubt about the importance of their wire!
a) Would you agree with these manufacturers that, without barbed wire, the homesteaders could not have become prosperous?
Now read Source D.
b) Were the railroads as vital to the development of the West as R. A. Billington clearly believes?
c) Is it possible to pick out *one* factor as being the most important in helping the development of the West? Explain your answer carefully.

SOURCE E

'Life, shut up in the little wooden farmhouses cannot well be very cheerful. A drive to the nearest town is almost the only diversion. There the farmers and their wives gather in the stores and manage to enjoy a little sociability. . . .

There are few social events in the life of these prairie farmers to enliven the monotonony of the long winter evenings; no singing schools, spelling schools, debating clubs, or church gatherings. Neighbourly calls are infrequent because of the long distances which separate farmhouses.'

(*Atlantic Monthly* journal, 1893)

SOURCE F

'Our neighborhood people were a fine class of people. Social gatherings were common and the lunches of fried chicken, cake and delicacies. The sod school house had given way to a small frame building just before we arrived. . . . This house became the public hall for all entertainments, social gatherings, Sunday School and religious services.'

(C. G. Barns, *The Sod House*)

3 Sources E and F both describe the ways in which the homesteaders spent their spare time.
a) What are the main differences between the two sources on this point?
b) Using your knowledge of the ways in which the Great Plains were settled, explain how it could be possible for *both* sources to be correct.
c) Source E was written for a magazine published in the eastern states of America. Source F was written by Dr C. G. Barns, who, as you have seen, was a young doctor on the Plains in 1878.
Would an historian consider that Source E gave a less reliable picture of life on the Plains than Source F?

SOURCE G

'There came through yesterday two old-fashioned mover wagons headed east . . . . [They had] four horses, very poor and very tired, one mule, more disheartened than the horses, and one sad-eyed dog. A few farm implements of the simpler sort were loaded in the wagon. . . . All the rest of the impedimenta [*their belongings*] had been left on the battlefield, and these poor stragglers, defeated but not conquered, were fleeing to another field, to try the fight again. For ten years they had been fighting the elements. They have tossed through hot nights, wild with worry, and have arisen only to find their worst nightmares grazing in reality on the brown stubble in front of their sun-warped doors. They had such high hopes when they went out there.'

(*The Gazette*, a Kansas newspaper, 1895)

4 By the 1890s the Great Plains had become prosperous farmlands. Can you explain, then, why this report (Source G) should appear in a Kansas newspaper in 1895?

Manifest destiny

In the introduction to this book you read how force, treaties and money had enabled the United States, by 1853, to own the whole of the continent of America from the Atlantic to Pacific coast and from the Canadian to the Mexican border. Americans were, however, afraid that they would not be able to hold on to this land which was theirs. They were afraid that Great Britain, France or Mexico would change their minds and try to take back the land which they had made over to the United States. One solution to this problem would be to fill these lands with men and women who were loyal to the young United States, and not to the older countries of Great Britain, France and Mexico. These men and women would, it was argued, build homesteads and towns, railways and roads, and would farm, mine and trade. They would thus make a takeover by another country extremely difficult. They would help to make the United States strong and prosperous, and safe from any enemies.

This was, of course, just one solution to the problem. However, it was a solution which quickly became part of a dream. This dream had begun to grow in the minds of Americans even before they gained their independence from Great Britain. This was the dream that the whole of the American continent would be settled by white Americans. Gradually they came to believe that this was the right and natural thing to happen. Not only was it right and natural, but it was something which clearly *had* to happen. It was their manifest destiny.

Thus when the wagon trains rolled westwards, and when the homesteaders began settling the Great Plains, Americans believed that the migrants were not simply looking for new and fertile farmland. They were putting the American dream into action. They were beginning the final wave of migration which would end with the whole of America being lived in by white Americans. They believed that civilization would be brought to the wilderness, and to the savage Indians who lived there. The manifest destiny of the American people was being fulfilled.

'Westward the course of Empire takes its way': a painting by Emanuel Leutze, 1861

SOURCE WORK: Manifest destiny

SOURCE A

BUFFALO JERKY

Slice buffalo meat along the grain into strips $\frac{1}{8}$ inch thick, $\frac{1}{2}$ inch wide and 2 to 3 inches long. Hang them on a rack in a pan and bake at 200° until dry. To prepare outside, suspend them over a fire or drape them on bushes to dry in the sun.

SODA BREAD

To make dough, mix 1 teaspoon of baking soda with 1 cup of warm water, add $2\frac{1}{4}$ cups of flour and 1 teaspoon of salt. Knead well. The dough may be used at once or allowed to rise overnight in a warm place. In either case, flatten dough to a thickness of 1 inch. Place on a greased cookie sheet and bake (in a 400° oven) for about 25 minutes.

MORMON JOHNNYCAKE

Combine 2 cups of yellow cornmeal, $\frac{1}{2}$ cup of flour, 1 teaspoon baking soda, and 1 teaspoon salt. Stir in 2 cups of buttermilk and 2 tablespoons of molasses. Pour batter into a greased 9-inch pan and bake (in a 425° oven) for about 20 minutes. Cut into 16 squares. To make lighter cake; add 2 beaten eggs and 2 tablespoons of melted butter to buttermilk and cook about 25 minutes.'

(H. Horn, *The Pioneers*)

1 These recipes were never actually used by the early pioneers. They are modernised versions of what the pioneers might have cooked. Why would present day Americans want to eat the same sort of food as that eaten by the early pioneers?

SOURCE B

'I saw that a great American community would grow up, in the space of a few years, upon the shores of the distant Pacific. At that time the country was claimed by both Great Britain and the United States. The only way to settle the matter was to fill the country with American citizens. If we could only show, by a practical test, that American emigrants could safely make their way across the continent to Oregon with their wagons, teams, cattle and families, then there would be no doubt as to who owned the country.'

(P. H. Burnett, *Recollections and Opinions of an Old Pioneer*, in *The Quarterly of the Oregon History Society* (Vol. 5 No. 1), March 1904

2 Look at the picture opposite. In 1860 the American Congress asked the artist to paint a picture which was supposed to show the spirit of the early pioneers and homesteaders. It is a mural, and is painted on one of the walls of the Capitol building in Washington.
   Now read Source B, which was written by an old man who had once been a pioneer. In what ways is the painting illustrating the same sort of feelings that the old man is describing?

3 Now look at the photograph on page 74 of this chapter which shows homesteaders moving into Nebraska in a covered wagon. Look again at the painting opposite. Do you think that the painting or the photograph better shows the spirit of the men and women who crossed and who settled the Great Plains?

4 Look carefully at the front cover of this book. It shows a painting which, like the picture opposite, is also called 'Westward the course of Empire takes its way'.
   a) What are the differences between the two paintings?
   b) Which of the paintings, in your opinion, best shows how the United States spread westwards?

5 One hundred years after Emanuel Leutze painted his picture (opposite) it was described as:'Civilisation approaches the Indian with a bottle in one hand, a treaty in the other, a bludgeon under her arm and a barrel of whiskey in her wagon.'
   Would you agree that this was, in fact, how the American West was settled? (It might be best to answer this question when you have finished the chapter 'The struggle for the Plains'.)

6

LAW AND ORDER

The Wild West?

The Wild West! Bandits, gunslingers, cattle rustlers and trigger-happy cowboys! The names of Wyatt Earp, Jesse James, Wild Bill Hickok, Billy the Kid and Calamity Jane are part of the legend of the West. Was it as wild and as violent as the stories and the films would have us believe?

The main problems in law and order arose in those areas which were growing, but had not long been organised. It took time to set up effective governments in new territories. This was especially true when they covered vast areas of land, and were far away from fully organised states, such as California and the states east of the Mississippi. Even when the system had been set up, it did not always work properly. Men who were supposed to keep law and order were not always honest. Criminals were often able to outwit even honest lawmen.

Problems of law and order in the mining regions

At the time of the 1848–9 gold rush in California (see Chapter 3) men were quick to take the law into their own hands to deal with criminals who tried to rob and swindle honest gold-diggers. They set up their own miners' courts to deal with problems like this.

Most of the early miners were law-abiding. Some individuals and groups, however, were violent and disruptive. The miners' courts found that they could not deal with these. Citizens were often so concerned that they set up Vigilance Committees. These Vigilance Committees took the law into their own hands. They held instant trials, after which many a condemned man would be seen hanging from a nearby tree.

The idea of vigilance groups spread, especially in areas where there was no properly organised law. In the second gold rush of 1858–9, when gold was discovered in the mountain areas which were to become Colorado and Nevada, robbery, fraud and violence were also problems. The desperate rush to find gold attracted men who were not as law-abiding as the first gold-diggers.

Gold strikes followed in other, nearby regions, and hundreds of people flocked to the mining camps. These camps were in organised territory but they were usually on the far edges of large Federal terri-

tories, so there was rarely any effective government there.

The main difficulties in the mining areas were to do with gold and claims to land. There were no laws to authorise mining in these areas or to give legal ownership to those who claimed land. Miners were, therefore, trespassing on public domain (see Chapter 5). This led to claim jumping, when men would simply seize land which had been claimed by others. Anger and violence often followed. Gold attracted not only the honest miner but also the swindler, the robber and the con-man. These had to be kept in check somehow.

Miners' courts were set up in Colorado and Nevada, just as they had been some ten years earlier in California. The places were different, but the problems were similar. The miners' courts could not deal with the worst cases and so vigilance groups were set up to hand out instant justice.

The people of Bannack (Montana) were being terrorised by a gang of 100 road agents (or highwaymen). They used to rob miners and other travellers on the road. They were a well organised gang. They even wore special knots in their ties so that they could recognise each other. It gradually became clear that the man who had been elected sheriff in Bannack, Henry Plummer, a well respected member of the community, was the leader of this gang. A Vigilance Committee was started, and one of the gang confessed all. Plummer tried to escape, but was caught and hung by the vigilantes in 1864.

The vigilantes were clearly needed to deal with cases like these, and they were very successful in clearing the mining areas of individuals and gangs who terrorised honest citizens.

Were the vigilantes necessary?

On the other hand, people in the camps and the towns sometimes feared the vigilantes themselves. The editor of the newspaper, the *Idaho World* gave some idea of feeling against the vigilantes when he wrote, on 2 September 1865: 'The remedy for the existing evils is greater than the evils'. The 'trials' which the vigilantes held were always too hasty for any real justice to be done, especially when it was clear what people wanted the verdict to be. There was no appeal from their verdict, either. It was all too easy to try and to execute anyone who got on the wrong side of an influential citizen.

Perhaps it was as well that the miners' courts and the vigilance groups were seen only as a temporary measure. It could only be a matter of time before the US Congress provided proper law enforcement measures. So miners in successful camps were only too eager to get their camps established with town governments.

Unfortunately, even when law and order had been organised locally, it did not always work properly. County sheriffs often had very large areas to cover, and town marshals often had far too much work to do. Even worse, local people were not always prepared to pay for the services which were needed to organise the town properly. Criminals and road gangs always seemed to know where they could strike without fear of being caught! It is not surprising, then, that vigilance groups appeared again, issuing dire warnings to all who disturbed the peace.

SOURCE WORK: Mining towns and vigilantes

SOURCE A

'These were dark days in Bannack; there was no safety for life or property only so far as each individual could, with his trusty rifle, protect his own. The respectable citizens far outnumbered the desperadoes, but having come from all corners of the earth, they were unacquainted and did not know whom to trust. On the other hand the 'Roughs' were organised and under the able leadership of that accompliced villain, Henry Plummer. At times it would seem that they had the upper hand and would run affairs to suit themselves.'

(G. Stuart, *Forty Years on the Frontier Vol. 1*)

SOURCE B

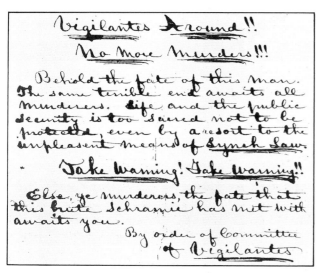

A vigilante warning found pinned to the body of a man lynched for murder. Lynch law is punishment, and even execution, without a proper trial

1 Read Sources A and B.
  a) Why were there problems of law and order in the mining communities even when they had been organised into territories?
  b) How do these sources help to show why vigilance groups were necessary?
  c) Now read pages 92–3 again. How does this help to explain why vigilance groups came to be feared as much as those whom they set out to punish?

SOURCE C

'Justice and protection from wrong to person and to property are the birthright of every American citizen. . . . These must be [provided] by constitutional law whenever . . . provision can be made for its enforcement. But when justice is powerless as well as blind . . . "self preservation is the first law of nature".'

(Prof. T. J. Dimsdale, *The Vigilantes of Montana*, University of Oklahoma Press 1865)

2 Professor Dimsdale, who lived in Montana, is here justifying the existence of vigilance groups. Using your knowledge of the events of the time, do you think that the citizens of places like Bannack or Montana would have agreed with him?

Gunslingers and gangs

Most of the legendary shoot-outs of the Wild West are set in the cow-towns of the mid-West, like Dodge City. There is no doubt that there were trigger-happy gangs and high-spirited cowboys in these towns. It is doubtful, though, whether it was all quite as glamorous or even as violent as the books and the films would lead us to believe. A saloon may indeed have erupted into violence, as a cowboy with money to gamble away lost his temper and drew his gun on a card-cheat.

There were, also, without doubt, bank and train robberies. Butch Cassidy and the Sundance Kid were not just invented for the cinema screen!

There was, however, not always very much difference between a law-man like Wyatt Earp and a gunslinger like Jesse James. Earp lasted for two years in Wichita, serving under the marshal and his assistants before he was arrested, fined and fired for disturbing the peace! Wichita itself had quite a reputation for disorder, too!

On the other hand, Thomas Smith, who became marshal of Abilene in 1870, managed to clean up the town within his first year. He was respected, feared and reasonably honest. Yet he was murdered later in 1870 whilst trying to make an arrest outside Abilene. Violence was never far below the surface.

Frank and Jesse James were widely known as bank robbers. They were born in Missouri, and after the Civil War they formed a band which specialised in train and bank robberies. They managed to escape the law until 1882. Then, Jesse was shot in the back by Bob Ford, one of his own gang who was after the reward which you can see promised in this poster.

Bank robbers, however, were not really unpopular, since banks were considered to be there only for the rich. The really unpopular criminals were the cattle-rustlers. There was far more violence in the Range Wars between the cattlemen and the homesteaders than in the cow-towns between gunslingers and lawmen.

A reward (left) is offered for the capture of the James gang 'dead or alive'. You can see how the James gang (below) is made to look sinister and watchful in this painting. Stories of the daring exploits of the gang spread across America and have lasted to this day, though the truth is probably less than the legend. Over the years the James gang probably pulled in only $2000 a year for each man, which is nothing like the huge wealth they were supposed to have gained

REWARD!
- DEAD OR ALIVE -

$5,000.⁰⁰ will be paid for the capture of the men who robbed the bank at

NORTHFIELD, MINN.

They are **believed** to be Jesse James and his Band, or the **Youngers**.

All officers are **warned** to use precaution in making arrest. **These are the most desperate men in America.**

Take no chances! Shoot to kill!!

J. H. McDonald,
SHERIFF

SOURCE WORK: Gunslingers and gangs

SOURCE A

'I have been in a good many towns but Newton is the fastest one I have ever seen. Here you may see young girls not over sixteen drinking whisky, smoking cigars, cursing and swearing until one almost loses the respect they should have for the weaker sex. I heard one of their townsmen say that he didn't believe there were a dozen virtuous women in town. This speaks well for a town of 1500 inhabitants. He further told me if I had any money that I would not be safe with it here. It is a common expression that they have a man every morning for breakfast.'

(*The Wichita Tribune*, 1860s)

SOURCE B

'The "Cattle Towns" at the head of the trails have been glorified in film and fiction as models of unbridled corruption where dance halls, bawdy houses [*brothels*], and gambling saloons lined the streets and shoot-outs were of such common occurence that the local "boot hills" [*burial places for cowboys*] received new customers daily. Two of them – Ellsworth and Dodge City – did gain an unenviable reputation for lawlessness, but only during their early years before the cattle trade began, when buffalo hunters and bad men concentrated there. This changed as soon as the trade attracted a group of merchants interested in profits. They wanted law-enforcement, but they recognised also that cowboys needed relaxation at the end of the long drive, and that unduly harsh punishment for wrongdoers would cause ill-feeling among the drovers, and with it a possible loss of trade. Hence saloons and dance halls were allowed, but not in excessive numbers; Abilene during its busiest season boasted no more than eleven taverns, Ellsworth ten, and Dodge City eight.'

(R. A. Billington, *Westward Expansion*)

SOURCE C

'Ordinances [*rules*] against carrying guns were in force in all Cattle Towns; between 1870 and 1885 only forty-five men were killed (including sixteen by police) and of these thirty-nine died of gun-shot wounds, not six-shooters. Only twice were as many as five men killed during a single year – in Ellsworth in 1873 and in Dodge City five years later. The "shoot-out" glorified in "western" stories and motion pictures was unheard of. In all the Cattle Towns only three men were executed for crimes and one was lynched; not one of these was a cowboy and none convicted of gun fighting or a shooting affair.'

(R. A. Billington, *Westward Expansion*)

SOURCE D

'In 1968, Robert Dykstra in his fine [book] *Cattle Towns* claimed that only forty-five killings occurred between 1870 and 1885 and only a few were directly caused by gun-fights between lawmen and cowboys. But since then others have suggested that the total was far higher, especially in Dodge City and Newton.'

(R. May, *The Story of the Wild West*, Hamlyn 1978)

2 In what ways do Sources A, C and D *agree* about: i) gun-fights? ii) deaths? iii) the keeping of law and order in the cattle towns?

3 a) What evidence is there in Sources A-D, and this section of the chapter, that historians disagree about the state of law and order in the cattle towns of the West?

(b) Why do you think historians disagree over this?

(c) *Westward Expansion* (see Sources B and C) is a secondary source. Does this mean that it is likely to be less reliable as evidence about law and order in the cow-towns than the *Wichita Tribune* (Source A)? Explain your answer carefully.

1 Read Sources A and B. In what ways does Source B (i) support and (ii) contradict source A?

SOURCE WORK: The shoot-out at the OK Corral

The shoot-out at the OK Corral on 26 October 1881 is probably one of the best-known stories of the Wild West, and there is no doubt that it actually happened. Virgil Earp was town marshal of Tombstone, Arizona. His deputies were his brothers Wyatt and Morgan. These three, with dentist lawman, 'Doc' Holliday, gunned down Tom and Frank McLowry and Billy Clanton. You can see where this took place on the street plan of Dodge City (Source A).

Not all versions of the story are the same, as you can see from the Sources below. The truth was that bank robbers were often more popular than the marshals and the deputies who gunned them down. The Earps became very unpopular after the shoot-out. They were even accused of cold-blooded murder.

SOURCE A

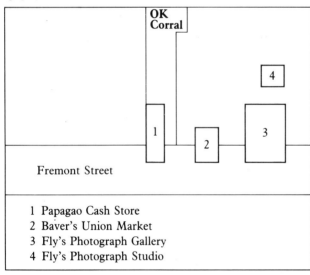

1 Papagao Cash Store
2 Baver's Union Market
3 Fly's Photograph Gallery
4 Fly's Photograph Studio

Part of Dodge City, showing the area surrounding the OK Corral

SOURCE B

'On the morning of October 26, Ike Clanton was back in Tombstone, with his younger brother Billy, Frank and Tom McLowry, and Billy Claiborne, all men with reputations as cattle rustlers. Virgil Earp, now assistant marshal, deputized his brothers Wyatt and Morgan, and the three patrolled the streets, apparently trying to pick a quarrel with the Clantons: Virgil struck Ike . . . and Wyatt

punched Tom McLowry. When the Clantons went to the OK Corral to collect their horses and leave town, the Earp brothers followed them. Doc Holliday tagged along with a sawed-off shotgun under his frock-coat.

In the corral, Virgil called out, "You are under arrest". Somebody fired. In less than a minute, Billy Clanton and the McLowrys were dead, Ike Clanton and Billy Claiborne had run for their lives, Morgan Earp had a bullet in the left shoulder, Virgil one in the leg, and Holliday one in the left hip. When the Clanton and McLowry bodies were laid out in their caskets, citizens hung a large notice over them: "Murdered in the streets of Tombstone".'

(B. Innes, 'The Wild West', in *The Wild West*, ed. H. S. Commager, Grolier Enterprises 1976)

SOURCE C

'[This] is best told in the words of R. F. Coleman, who was an eyewitness from the beginning to the end. Mr Coleman says: I was in the OK Corral at 2.30 p.m., when I saw the two Clantons Ike and Bill, and the two McLowry boys . . . in earnest conversation across the street. I went up the street and notified Sheriff Beban, and told him it was my opinion they meant trouble, and that it was his duty, as Sheriff, to go and disarm them. . . . I then went and saw Marshal Virgil Earp and notified him to the same effect. I then . . . walked through the OK Corral about fifty yards behind the Sheriff. On reaching Fremont St I saw Virgil Earp, Wyatt Earp, Morgan Earp and Doc Holliday in the centre of the street, all armed. I went along to Fry's photograph gallery, when I heard Virgil Earp say, "Give up your arms, or throw up your arms". There was some reply made by Frank McLowry, but at the same moment there were two shots fired simultaneously by Doc Holliday and Frank McLowry. The firing then became general, over thirty shots being fired. Tom McLowry fell first, but raised and fired again before he died. Bill Clanton fell next, and raised to fire again when Mr Fly [*the owner of a photograph gallery and shop on Fremont Street*] took his revolver from him.

Frank McLowry ran a few rods [*a short way*] and fell. Morgan Earp was shot through and fell. Doc Holliday was hit in the left hip, but kept on firing. Virgil Earp was hit in the third or fourth fire in the leg, which staggered him, but he kept up his effective work. Wyatt Earp stood up and fired in rapid succession, as cool as a cucumber, and was not hit. . . . After the firing was over Sheriff Beban went up to Wyatt Earp and said, "I'll have to arrest you". Wyatt replied, "I won't be arrested today. I am right here and am not going away. You have deceived me; you told me those men were disarmed; I went to disarm them." '

(*The Daily Epitaph*, Tombstone, Arizona, 27 October, 1881)

SOURCE D

'It was October 26, 1881. The outlaws were lined up against the wall of the Assay Office backing onto the corral . . . Tom McLowery was the nearest to the street. Then came his brother, Frank, the most dangerous gunslinger in the lot, and teen-aged Billy Clanton, and his brother Ike. Billy Claiborne, wearing a Colt on either hip, was on the other end of the line. The quintet [were] tense and alert, eyes glued on the point where the corral opened out into Tombstone's Fremont Street.

In a moment the men they were waiting for came into view. Wyatt and Virgil Earp turned the corner first, then Morgan Earp and Doc Holliday. The tall, handsome Earps wore black from head to foot, the sombre design broken only by their white shirts. Holliday had on a black frock coat . . . and under it bulged a sawn-off shot gun. "You men are under arrest", Virgil Earp sang out as his party moved within eight feet of the lean, desert-hardened outlaws. "Throw up your hands."

Suddenly guns roared in the crisp, bright afternoon, as the greatest face to face, wide-open gunfight in the history of the West – the Battle of the OK Corral – got under way.

Frank McLowery fell first. A slug from Wyatt Earp's Buntline Special tore into him just above his gunbelt. Morgan Earp, his coat singed by a bullet from Tom McLowery's .45, put a shot into Billy Clanton's gun hand as the youth poured fire at Wyatt. Billy Claiborne fled. Ike Clanton rushed up to Wyatt Earp. "Don't kill me! I'm not shooting!" "This

fight's commenced", Earp answered. "Get to fighting or get out." So Clanton got out, ducking into Fly's.

Now Tom McLowery's .45 found a mark. A slug ripped into Morgan Earp's left shoulder, but he kept fighting. Wyatt concentrated on Tom McLowery, who started to run. Both Holliday and Wyatt Earp hit him and he fell dead. His brother Frank, staggering as his life ebbed away, turned on Holliday. Morgan Earp saw it. Three pistols exploded at once. McLowery fell with bullets in his head and heart.

The dying Billy Clanton shot Virgil through the leg before Wyatt's gun brought him down.

The Battle of the OK Corral was over. It had taken less than thirty seconds.'

(Horan and Sann, *A Pictorial History of the Wild West*, Hamlyn 1954)

1 Read these three accounts of the gunfight at the OK Corral. They are long, but it is worth reading them carefully.
a) Make lists for yourself of the ways in which they *agree* or *disagree* on the main points of the story. You could, for example, look at
   i) where the battle took place in each account;
   ii) who fired at whom and who was supposed to have killed whom;
   iii) how long the battle took, and the amount of action which was supposed to have taken place within that time.
There will be other details which you will find for yourselves.
b) Now try to decide
   i) which account is the most exciting,
   ii) which account is the most balanced,
   iii) which account is the most biased.
c) Now you are going to use all the information which you gathered in your answer to (a), and your opinions in your answer to (b). You could also refer to the introduction to these sources opposite.
   i) Why do you think that there are different versions of the story?
   ii) What do you think happened? Were all the 'outlaws' armed? Were they spoiling for a fight? Did the Earps go out looking for a fight?
   iii) And, as the last word, why do you think the fight has become so famous?

The Johnson County War

Cattlemen and farmers in Wyoming

Wyoming became a territory in 1868, and a state in 1890. It was well organised and known to be peaceful, with honest and God-fearing people. Yet in 1892, in Johnson County, a fierce and bloody battle broke out between the two groups of inhabitants, the cattlemen and the farmers.

There had been trouble in Johnson County before. The Bozeman Trail to the goldfields of Montana had aroused the Sioux Indians, and caused Red Cloud's War of 1866–8, (see Chapter 7, pages 105–9). The Indians won the war, but the white men won the land in the end, and it became a successful cattle ranching area. The land was good, and so, in addition to the ranchers who set up there, homesteaders flooded in. They claimed land and began to farm it. The cattlemen, though, were richer than the farmers and had been there longer. They therefore had a good deal of power, locally and in the Federal Government. They had formed the influential Wyoming Stock Growers Association, to which the state governor belonged. Through this they managed to control the financial policy of the territory and to get laws passed which would serve their own interests.

The mid 1880s were disastrous years for ranchers all over the Plains (see Chapter 4). The cattlemen who survived these years bitterly resented the farmers who had taken land. When many ranchers became bankrupt, this left more land for the taking. So, in the mid 1880s, large numbers of 'sod-busters' came to claim this land.

Every time a farmer claimed land, especially if it was around a water-hole, and fenced it off, the cattlemen's anger and resentment grew. The farmers continued to fence their lands and to deny the cattlemen access to the water-holes. So the community became divided into two hostile bands. The fencing of the land, however was not the real cause of the trouble; it was cattle-rustling.

Cattle-rustling

Cattle-rustling, or cattle stealing, was always a problem for cattlemen. There is no doubt that this happened in Wyoming, but the ranchers' charge that all the rustling was done by the farmers was probably unjust. Most of the farmers were hard-working folk who just wanted to make an honest living. Some of them, however, might have rustled the occasional cow. The Stock Growers' Association hired gunfighters to root out the rustlers. Their chief was Frank Canton, one-time sheriff of Johnson County, ex-bank robber and killer.

Soon the cattlemen had the first 'proof' of this rustling. Just outside Johnson County lived Ella Watson and Jim Averill. Jim Averill ran a small store, saloon and post office. Ella Watson, with whom he lived, was a Canadian whore from Kansas who took in visiting cowboys. The problem was that the cowboys often paid in cattle rather than in money. It could certainly have looked as if the cattle had been rustled! It was unfortunate for Jim and Ella that they lived on land which was used by a rancher named Albert Bothwell. He was very angry about a letter which Jim Averill had written to the *Weekly Mail* in April 1889, which said that the rich ranchers were nothing but land-grabbers. In July, Bothwell and some of his friends arrived at Jim and Ella's cabin, and hanged them up beside each other on a nearby tree. There had been no trial.

Ella Watson and Jim Averill hanging, Wyoming 1889

Ella Watson is remembered as 'Cattle Kate the Rustler Queen'. Was she a clever rustler or was she merely a harmless whore? In the photograph opposite, she looks harmless enough – but who can tell! What is certain is that she looks a good deal older in the photograph than she does in the picture above.

Jim Averill (left) and Ella Watson (right), shortly before she was hanged. Why do you think they look so different in the photographs and in the drawing?

The Johnson County War

Other killings followed, many of which were of innocent people. The rustling continued. The Association's next move was to draw up a list of about seventy wanted rustlers. Some of them may have been honest settlers; some of them may have been rustlers. They then formed a Vigilance Committee called the Regulators. The homesteaders decided to arm themselves and they elected as sheriff 'Red' Angus, who had some sympathy for their cause.

In April 1892 Wyoming was invaded by the hired gunmen and some local men, led by Major Frank Wolcott and Frank Canton. The *Denver News* produced this account of the battle which followed.

'Forty-six men killed in Wyoming yesterday.

Nate Champion and 50 men are surrounded by 100 men at the T. A. ranch. Two hundred shots have been discharged, but the damage done on either side cannot be ascertained.

A number of men are known to have been wounded and some killed. About 100 rustlers have passed through town en route to the scene of the battle to help Champion and his men.'

A homesteader had seen Champion's death, and realised that the 'invaders' were on their way to get the rustlers. He took the news to the nearby town, Buffalo. The citizens were outraged. Sheriff Angus, getting no help from the military at the nearby Fort McKinney, or from the National Guard, organised

a posse to ride out to arrest the invaders. The invaders were now heading for Buffalo. Hearing that the town was up in arms, most of the ranchers decided to make for the TA ranch and dig themselves in.

The ranch was surrounded by angry settlers, led by 'Red' Angus. Word soon got through to the Governor and even to Benjamin Harrison, President of the USA. The President thought that the whole of Johnson County was in a state of rebellion and ordered troops to be sent to restore peace. Three days after the seige had begun the ranchers surrendered to the US forces. In return the forces promised that they would not hand over the ranchers to the authorities at Buffalo. Instead they were taken to the civil authorities at Cheyenne, where they were well known and amongst friends.

There was no real victory for either side. The invaders were let off, but the homesteaders could also claim a victory, since they stayed. The ranchers, too began to enclose their ranges. In a sense, the end of the range wars was also the end of the open range.

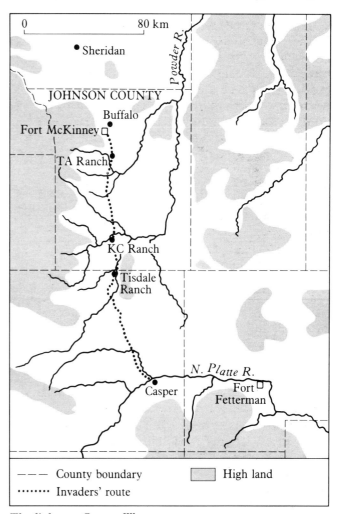

The Johnson County War

7

THE STRUGGLE FOR THE PLAINS

By the 1880s the Great Plains were no longer the Great American Desert. They had, first of all, been crossed by early settlers and miners. Then they had seen cattle trails and railroads. Finally they had been settled and farmed successfully by homesteaders. We have not yet seen, however, how the Indians who lived and hunted in these areas reacted to white Americans and the 'iron horse' – the railroad. In this chapter you can find out what happened to the Indians whom you met in Chapter 2: the north-western mountain tribes such as the Nez Perces and the Shoshonis; the warlike Apaches and the Navahos of the south-western mountains; and the Indians of the Plains such as the Cheyennes and the Sioux.

The Indians fought fiercely to defend their home-lands, but they were unable to defeat the white Americans' determination to push the frontier west-ward. As early as the 1840s Francis Parkman could imagine what would happen to the Plains in the future – and he was only looking at the early pioneers who crossed the Plains, not at those who settled on them:

> 'With the stream of emigration to Oregon and California, the buffalo will dwindle away, and the large wandering communities who depend on them for support must be broken and scattered. The Indians will soon be ruined by whiskey and over-awed by military posts; so that within a few years the traveller may pass in tolerable security through their country. Its danger and its charm will have disappeared altogether.'

It is not difficult to understand how the Indians felt about the loss of their lands and of their way of life. Nevertheless, we should also try to understand the feelings and the ambitions of the white Americans who wanted to move into these areas.

White Americans and Indians: early days

The first Indians who made it difficult for white Americans to gain more lands were those living in the eastern states. Ever since the days of the first white settlers, in the sixteenth century, white people had been buying land from Indians in exchange for money, guns or other goods. Some of the tribes in the eastern states even began to try to live like white Americans and took up farming. Some learned to read and write. They hoped that they would be able to stay on their lands if they behaved like white people. This was just not possible. Land-hungry settlers wanted the Indians out, but where could they send them?

West of the Mississipi lay the 'Louisiana Purchase', the huge area which President Thomas Jefferson had bought from the French in 1803. This was the Great American Desert, where it was thought no white people would ever settle. It was here that the eastern Indians would be forced to move and make way for white American people. The so-called 'Five Civilised Tribes' – the Cherokees, Creeks, Chickasaws, Choc-taws and Seminoles – were moved from the south-east to an area on the eastern fringe of the Great Plains, which is now the state of Oklahoma. This was to be Indian Territory.

The Permanent Indian Frontier

The move began in 1825. In 1832 a special govern-ment department was set up to deal with Indian affairs. It soon decided that the whole of the Great Plains could be given to the Indian tribes. The Great American Desert would be 'One Big Reservation' behind the 95th meridian, which was to be the Permanent Indian Frontier. By 1840 all the other tribes had been moved from their eastern lands into this new Indian Territory.

The Government thought that their new lands beyond the Permanent Indian Frontier had all that the Indians would want, but could provide nothing for white people. How wrong they were! Very soon miners, Mormons and other settlers were moving across the Plains in search of new lands. Sometimes the Indians attacked these travellers who were taking their lands and disturbing their way of life. By 1850 it was clear that the problem was far greater than anyone had imagined: the Frontier was fast crum-bling, and white Americans were faced with thinking of a new policy for the Indians.

Settlers move west: the Indian policy changes

The mountain Indians

White people who crossed the Plains were soon demanding protection from Indian attacks, and miners were not prepared to let Indians stop them digging for gold and silver. The northern mountain Indians, like the Snakes, the Bannacks and the Ute, did not present much of a problem. They were not warlike, and did not hunt or live off the buffalo. By 1868 most of these tribes had agreed to move to special areas.

The south-western mountain Indians, like the Apaches and the Navahos, were more troublesome. They were warlike and much feared. They resisted anyone who tried to drive them off their lands. By 1868, however, even they had been forced to give in to the army. The Navahos finally agreed to go to an area by Fort Sumner on the Pecos River, and to become farmers. The Apaches were moved to New Mexico and Arizona between 1871 and 1874.

The Plains Indians

The Plains Indians proved to be much more troublesome than any other nation or tribe of Indians. They were gifted horsemen and skilful fighters. They were also wandering hunters, who needed to be able to wander freely to follow the herds of buffalo. On the other hand, white people needed to be able to travel without fear of attack. Some of the Plains Indians had shown friendliness to whites, and were less warlike than others. The Arapahos of the southern Plains were not normally hostile, and the Kiowas and the Kiowa-Apaches were usually reluctant to fight. It was only because there was an increasing number of white people taking the trails to the West in the 1840s and 1850s that the Plains Indians began to attack the smaller wagon trains and the mail coaches.

In 1849 the Government made treaties with the Comanches and the Kiowas. The Indians agreed to allow United States citizens across their lands and to stop attacking travellers on the Santa Fe Trail. This was to be the new policy. Indians and white men signed treaties whereby the Indians promised not to attack travellers, traders or miners, in return for protection and guaranteed land.

The Fort Laramie Treaty, 1851

In the central Great Plains, around the North and South Platte and the Arkansas Rivers, lived the Cheyennes and the Arapahos. As more and more travellers took the Oregon Trail through their lands and joined in the California gold rush of 1849 the Indians became very restless and started to attack the wagon trains. Other tribes, too, were making more frequent attacks on the wagon trains. In 1851 Thomas Fitzpatrick, the Indian agent controlling the Platte River outpost, called together the chiefs of the main Plains tribes for a meeting near Fort Laramie. Fitzpatrick realised that the Indians were being threatened by the slaughter of buffalo by emigrants and miners, by diseases and by the whisky which white settlers brought with them. He feared that, unless some agreement was made, there would be a terrible war between Indians and white men.

Fitzpatrick's job was to get the Indians to sign a treaty agreeing to settle only in certain areas of the Plains. Each tribe would have its own hunting grounds, away from the trails, and from other tribes. The Oregon Trail would then be kept open and safe. The Government would also be able to open up former Indian land for white settlers who were beginning to move on to the eastern Plains. The Indians agreed to the terms of the Treaty which gave them lands – supposedly for ever – along the foothills of the Rockies between the North Platte and Arkansas. You can see on the map on the next page where the different tribes were sent. The Indians agreed to allow roads and military posts to be built, in return for government protection and $50,000 a year for ten years. This policy became known as 'concentration', because the Indians were 'concentrated', or put together, in certain areas. The days of the 'One Big Reservation' were over.

The Indians did not realise just what a clever move this was by the Government. If the tribes were separated it would be much easier to force one group to give up its land to the Government in the future, when settlers demanded more and more land. Separation would prevent other tribes from being aroused to support others whose lands were threatened.

Gold in Colorado!

Even the new policy of treaties and 'concentration' was not, in the end, the answer to the Indian problem. Within a few years of the Fort Laramie Treaty the attacks began again. The trouble started in Colorado, where the Cheyennes and the Arapahos had settled. In 1859 gold was discovered at Pike's Peak in the Colorado Mountains. In the rush for gold, the white men who surged through the Cheyenne and Arapaho lands forgot agreements made with the Indians. The Indians, however, remembering the white Americans' promises, soon took their revenge. By now, too, not only miners but also settlers had begun to move onto Indian lands in Kansas and Nebraska. The Indians were being pressed on all sides – by the miners from the West and the farmers from the East. In addition to this, railroad companies were demanding the removal of Indians and buffalo from the routes along which they were to build the railroads across the Plains. Then, in 1861, Colorado became a territory. It now officially belonged to white Americans.

The Arapahos and the Cheyennes now began serious attacks on railroad surveyors and travellers. In 1861 the Government called the chiefs from these tribes to a conference at Fort Lyon. Government officials forced them to abandon claims to the land given to them at Fort Laramie in 1851. Instead, they were to have a small reservation between the Arkansas River and Sand Creek in eastern Colorado. Indian chiefs, however, had no power to force their people to do anything. Many warriors refused to accept what their chiefs had agreed. They went on the war-path and raided mining camps and attacked mail coaches in Colorado and New Mexico. Even worse, only six out of forty-four Cheyenne chiefs were present for the signing of the Fort Lyon Treaty.

The carefully worked-out treaties had not solved the problem. What was to be the solution? Before anything could be done, there were to be several years of fierce warfare, as the Plains Indians resisted the attempts of white people to take from them the lands which had been given to them 'for ever' by the United States Government.

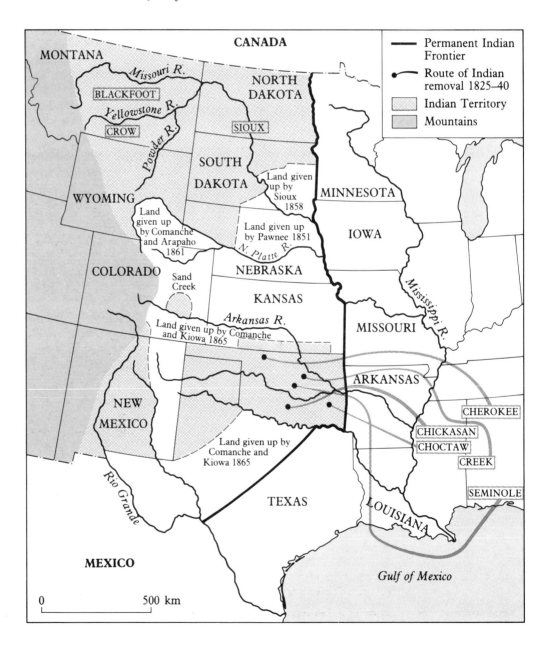

Lands of the Plains Indians in 1865

SOURCE WORK: White Americans and Indians: early days

SOURCE A

'They were ill-looking fellows, thin and swarthy, with care-worn anxious faces, and lips rigidly compressed. . . . Since leaving the settlements they had met with nothing but misfortune. Some of their party had died; one man had been killed by the Pawnees; and about a week before they had been plundered by the Dahcotahs [*Sioux*] of all their best horses.'

(F. Parkman, *The Oregon Trail*)

1 Look back to the section on the mountain men, on pages 38–9, and look also at Source A on page 39. Why, to begin with, were most Indians friendly towards white people, in the mountain areas and on the Plains?

2 Read Source A. This tells a different story.
   a) Read these suggestions about why Indian attacks on white people increased. Take each one and explain whether or not you agree with it:
      i) Some tribes, like the Blackfeet, were more hostile than others.
      ii) Francis Parkman was lying.
      iii) The Government encouraged travellers to kill Indians who came near wagon trains and camps.
      iv) Indians began to feel threatened as more and more white people crossed the Plains.
      v) Many travellers, like some miners, did not respect the rights of the Indians as the mountain men had done.
   b) Can you think of any other reasons?

SOURCE B

Extracts from the Treaty made at Fort Laramie on 17 September 1851:

'Article 1: The Indian nations to make an effective and lasting peace.
Article 2: The Indian nations do hereby recognise the right of the United States government to establish roads, military and other posts, within their territories.

Article 3: The United States bind themselves to protect the Indian nations against all depredations [*attacks to seize property or land*] by the people of the United States.
Article 5: [This Article described the lands which were to be given to the different Indian nations]
Article 7: The United States bind themselves to deliver to the Indian nations the sum of fifty thousand dollars per annum for the term of ten years in provisions, merchandise, domestic animals, and agricultural implements.'

(C. J. Kappler, *Indian Treaties*, Interland Publishing Inc. 1972)

SOURCE C

'To justify these breaches of the "permanent Indian frontier", the policy makers in Washington invented "Manifest Destiny". The Europeans and their descendants were ordained by destiny to rule all of America. They were the dominant race and therefore responsible for the Indians – along with their lands, their forests, and their mineral wealth.'

(Dee Brown, *Bury my Heart at Wounded Knee*)

3 The Treaty made at Fort Laramie in 1851 was an attempt to sort out the problems which had arisen between Indians and white people on the trails to the West.
   a) Which nations or tribes of Indians do you think the Treaty was mainly aimed at?
   b) Read Article 7. What was the Government trying to do by means of this Article?
   c) Do you think that the Government genuinely intended
      i) to protect the Indians?
      ii) to allow them to keep forever the lands given to them in the Treaty?
Use Source C and what you have learned from this chapter to help you to explain your answer. *You should base your answer only on evidence from the chapter and the sources, and make it as unbiased as possible.*

The Plains wars

The Sand Creek Massacre

In June 1864, after three years of raids and attacks, Governor Evans, the territorial governor of Colorado, ordered all warring bands to Fort Lyon. He threatened to kill them all if they refused. All this did was to make things worse; the attacks increased in number and became fiercer.

However, in August 1864, tired of the war and the killing, Black Kettle, a Cheyenne chief, tried to negotiate for peace with the federal commander at Fort Lyon, Major Edward Wynkoop. Wynkoop told Black Kettle that he could not end the fighting. He would, however, go with Black Kettle to Denver to speak to Governor Evans. He might be able to stop white men and Indians fighting. Wynkoop was wrong. When they arrived in Denver in late September 1864, Governor Evans refused to accept Black Kettle's surrender and to end the wars. 'What shall I do with the 3rd Colorado Regiment if I make peace?' he said. 'They have been raised to kill Indians and they must kill Indians.' Black Kettle returned and set up camp at Sand Creek.

In November, Wynkoop was replaced at Fort Lyon by Major Scott Anthony. Black Kettle went to see Anthony to ask for peace and protection. Anthony first promised him federal protection and then, uncertain that he had done the right thing, withdrew it and ordered Black Kettle from the fort. Black Kettle, believing that he would indeed be protected by federal troops, led his 700 Cheyenne to Sand Creek. Some Arapahos, who were camping close to Fort Lyon, decided to move away for safety. One band went to Sand Creek to join the Cheyennes. Little Raven, an Arapaho chief, took another band south across the Arkansas River.

In November a regiment of 1000 local volunteers under Colonel John Chivington arrived at the fort, eager to pursue Black Kettle. Chivington was told that the governor had not promised the Indians any sort of protection, and so he and his regiment set off for Sand Creek. They surrounded the camp, and at daybreak on 29 November 1864 they charged the camp. They took the Indians completely by surprise. Though Black Kettle raised the white flag and the Stars and Stripes, the regiment slaughtered over 450 Cheyennes and Arapahos – men, women and children. Black Kettle managed to escape, and carried news of the massacre to other tribes.

As a result of this, the Cheyennes, the Arapahos, the Comanches and the Kiowas increased their attacks on ranches, travellers and mail coaches throughout the winter of 1864–5. Any troops sent against them were resisted with bloody violence. What the Chivington massacre had done, however, was to horrify both white men and Indians; both now demanded an end to the wars. Even a government committee, which was looking at the massacre, declared:

'He deliberately planned and executed a foul and dastardly massacre which would have disgraced the most savage among those who were the victims of his cruelty.'

The meeting at Bluff Creek

A meeting was finally held at Bluff Creek, some 64 kilometres below the mouth of the Little Arkansas River, on 4 October 1865. A Peace Commission from the Government arrived to negotiate with the chiefs. The Cheyennes and the Arapahos agreed to lay down their arms and to give up Sand Creek, in return for lands in Indian Territory (Oklahoma), and money. Black Kettle, for the Cheyennes, and Little Raven, for the Arapahos, agreed to the terms on 14 October. On 17 October there was an agreement with the Kiowa-Apaches. On the day after, the Kiowas and the Comanches agreed to go to a reservation in north-western Texas, and to give up all claims to central Texas, western Kansas and eastern New Mexico.

There was, for a time at least, peace in the south-western plains, but it was not the end of the Plains Wars. The Sioux were still resisting the Government in the northern Plains – and this could break the fragile peace in the south-western Plains.

Fetterman's trap

In 1865 the US Government was planning to build a road to connect Virginia City, in the gold-fields of Montana, with Sioux City, on the Missouri. The trails which many of the miners had been taking had been long and roundabout, and they had asked for more direct routes. Jim Bridger, the wise and experienced 'mountain man', who had been hunting in the area for forty years (see Chapter 3), blazed a trail west of the Big Horns. He knew that the Sioux of the northern Plains wanted to keep white people out of their best hunting country, the foothills of the Big Horns. This area gave them plenty of grass and water, as well as buffalo, bear, deer, antelope and elk.

The Government, however, chose the trail which had been surveyed by John Bozeman, right through the Big Horn country. They were anxious to protect the miners from Indian attacks on the Bozeman Trail. They realised that this was the best route to

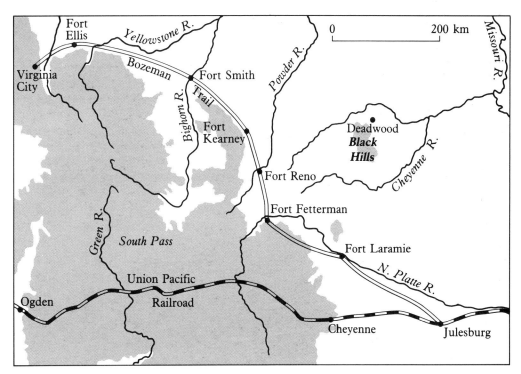

The Bozeman Trail

take to the goldfields, and so they decided to improve and protect it. The Sioux were worried, and, in the summer of 1865, the Sioux chief Red Cloud protested as the surveyors began their work. The Government warned Red Cloud that nothing would stand in the way of this road. To prove their point, they sent soldiers marching through the Big Horn country.

Indian attacks continued. In the autumn of 1865 the US Government signed peace treaties with the Indians, in which the Indians were guaranteed hunting rights in the area as long as they stopped attacking travellers on the trail. This still did not stop the attacks, and so, in the following year, troops began to build forts along the route of the proposed road; Fort Reno on the Powder River, Fort Philip Kearny north of this and Fort C. F. Smith where the Big Horn met the Powder River Road.

The troops who were building the forts were under constant Indian attack, and the situation reached breaking point in December 1866. Colonel Henry Carrington, who was in charge of the newly-established Montana District, knew that Red Cloud was determined not to come to terms with the white man. Yet he refused to mount an all-out attack on the Sioux. In November Captain William J. Fetterman had arrived with cavalry reinforcements. He had fought bravely and well in the Civil War, but he was arrogant and ambitious, and despised the more cautious Carrington for his policy towards the Indians. 'A single company of regulars could whip a thousand Indians', he said. 'Give me eighty men and I will ride through the Sioux nation.'

By now, however, it was not just the Sioux. Cheyenne and Arapaho warriors had joined Red Cloud in his fight against the white Americans. On 21 December a wood-train sent a message calling for help against an Indian attack. Carrington collected a small force to help, and Fetterman persuaded him to let him take part. Carrington was worried that Fetterman might take matters into his own hands, and so gave him written instructions saying:

'Support the wood-train. Relieve it and report to me. Do not engage or pursue Indians at its expense. Under no circumstances pursue over the ridge, that is, Lodge Trail Ridge.'

It seems that Fetterman had no intention of obeying orders. Instead of supporting the wood-train he and his men galloped after Indian horsemen along the Bozeman Trail and away from the fort. This was exactly what the Indians had planned. Fetterman had placed himself in the centre of a huge ring of Sioux, Cheyennes and Arapahos, who were hidden behind the tall grass and the rocks at the side of the Trail. The Indians attacked. The only survivors were Indians, including a young warrior called Crazy Horse. All eighty-two of Fetterman's men were killed.

The Fetterman disaster alarmed white Americans and delighted the Sioux. Indian attacks became fiercer and more frequent as Red Cloud became determined to drive away all white people from the area. Soon after, the Cheyennes attacked Fort C. F. Smith whilst the Sioux tried to take Fort Phil Kearney. There was no trap this time; the soldiers were ready, with their new breech-loading Springfield rifles which did not need to be re-loaded after each shot. Red Cloud lost many of his best warriors and called off the attack. It looked as if Red Cloud had lost the Sioux Wars, and that the Government would be able to ensure that white people could cross the Plains in safety.

SOURCE WORK: The Sand Creek Massacre

SOURCE A

This is an account of the Sand Creek Massacre by Robert Bent, the Cheyenne half-breed son of rancher William Bent. Robert Bent was forced by Chivington to go as a guide in the search for the Cheyenne camp.

'I saw the American flag waving and heard Black Kettle tell the Indians to stand around the flag, and there they were huddled – men, women and children. This was when we were within fifty yards of the Indians. I also saw a white flag raised. These flags were in so conspicuous a position that they must have been seen. I think there were six hundred Indians in all. I think there were thirty-five braves and some old men, about sixty in all. The rest of the men were away from camp, hunting. I saw five squaws under a bank for shelter. When the troops came up to them they ran out and begged for mercy, but the soldiers shot them all. I saw one squaw lying on the bank whose leg had been broken by a shell. A soldier came up to her with a drawn saber. She raised her arm to protect herself, when he struck, breaking her arm. She rolled over and raised her other arm, when he struck, breaking it, and then left her without killing her. There were some thirty or forty squaws collected in a hole for protection. They sent out a little girl about six years old with a white flag on a stick. She had not proceeded but a few steps when she was shot and killed. All the squaws in the hole were killed. Every one I saw dead was scalped. I saw quite a number of infants in arms killed with their mothers.'

(The US Congress 39th, 2nd session, Senate Report 156)

SOURCE B

An account of the Sand Creek Massacre given by Lieutenant James Connor.

'In going over the battleground the next day I did not see a body of man, woman, or child but was scalped, and in many instances their bodies were mutilated in the most horrible manner – men women and children's privates cut out etc. According to my best knowledge and belief these atrocities that were committed were with the knowledge of J. M. Chivington, and I do not know of his taking any measures to prevent them.'

(The US Congress 39th, 2nd session, Senate Report)

SOURCE C

An account by Stephen Decatur, Colorado Cavalryman.

'The next day after the battle I went over the battleground, and counted 450 dead Indian warriors. I took pleasure in going, as, the evening before, while the village was being burned, I saw something which made me feel as though I should have liked to have spent a little more time fighting. I saw some of the men opening bundles or bales. I saw them take therefrom a number of white persons' scalps – men's, women's and children's. I saw one scalp of a white woman in particular that I want to describe to you. The head had been skinned, taking all the hair. The scalp had been tanned to preserve it. The hair was auburn and hung in ringlets. It was very long hair.'

(The US Congress 39th, 2nd session, Senior Executive Document)

SOURCE D

An account given by Lieutenant Cramer.

'It was a mistake that there was any white scalps found in the village. I saw one but it was very old, the hair being much faded.
   We arrived at the Indian village about daylight. The women and the children were huddled together, and most of our fire was concentrated on them. The Indian warriors,

about one hundred in number, fought desperately. I estimated the loss of the Indians to be from one hundred and seventy-five killed. No wounded fell into our hands and all the dead were scalped.

I told Colonel Chivington that it would be murder if he attacked those Indians. His reply was, bringing his fist down close to my face, 'Damn any man who sympathises with Indians'. He had come to kill Indians and believed it to be honorable to kill any Indians under any and all circumstances.'

(The US Congress 39th, 2nd session, Senate Report)

1 Read Sources A, B, C and D. Make lists of what *each* source says about:
flags; numbers of warriors/braves; killing of women; killing of children; scalping of Indians; white scalps; mutilation of Indians; numbers of dead Indians.
   a) Which of the sources give *similar* accounts on these points? In what ways?
   b) Which of the accounts *differ* on these points? In what ways?
   c) Which of the accounts *contradict* each other on these points? In what ways?
   d) What reasons can you think of for any *differences* or *contradictions*?
   (Think about *who* wrote the sources or said the words and *why*. Remember that eye-witnesses do not always give similar accounts of the same event and that if sources differ it does not mean that one of them must be wrong.)

SOURCE E

Colonel Chivington, in a public speech made in Denver shortly before the massacre:

'Kill and scalp all, big and little. Nits make lice.'

2 How does this help to explain why the US soldiers killed Indian babies and children as well as adults?

SOURCE F

Now read this description of what an eye-witness felt when he saw the results of an attack by Indians on a US army division.

'I have seen in days gone by sights horrible and gory, but never did I feel the sickening sensation, the giddy, fainting feeling that came over me when I saw our dead, dying and wounded after this Indian fight. The bugler was stripped naked, and five arrows driven through him while his skull was literally smashed to atoms. Another soldier was shot with four bullets and three arrows, his scalp was torn off and his brains knocked out. Sergeant Wylyams lay dead beside the mangled horse. The muscles of the right arms, hacked to the bone, speak of the Cheyenne. The nose slit denotes the Arapaho. The cut throat bears witness that the Sioux were also present.'

(W. A. Bell, *New Tracks in North America, Vol. 1,* 1869)

3 Use any of the sources in this section to help you to answer this question, as well as what you have read in the chapter.
   Which of the following suggestions do you think best explains why the US soldiers scalped and mutilated Indians? Explain why you have chosen this one and not the others.
   a) Colonel Chivington ordered them to scalp the Indians.
   b) The Indians were dangerous and hostile.
   c) Indians scalped and mutilated white people.
   d) The soldiers enjoyed scalping and mutilating Indians.

4 Read the conclusion reached by the government committee which looked into the massacre (page 104 of this chapter). Do you agree with this? Remember to use the evidence which you have from the sources to help you to explain your answer.

5 'If it had not been for the US Army, it is possible that white people would never have been able to cross the Plains in safety.'
   a) Explain whether or not you agree with this suggestion.
   b) Would it have mattered if white people had never been able to cross the plains in safety?

A new policy

By 1867 many people were beginning to believe that a new policy towards the Indians was needed. More and more Americans were beginning to see that much of the trouble was caused by white people moving over and settling on territory which has been given to the Indians in the treaties after 1851. The Plains were no longer, as the Government had thought in the 1840s, useless to anyone but the Indians. Both Indians and white Americans had broken promises made in the treaties. Some Indian warriors had refused to accept the treaties. As we have seen, individual officers who were ambitious for fame and military glory took matters into their own hands with disastrous results. Many of the 'humanitarians' believed that the army should have a good deal less to do with the Indian problem, for violence and fighting only gave rise to more violence. This point of view was put to Congress in March, 1867, and a Peace Commission was set up to put together a final solution to the Indian problem.

This Commission agreed that the treaties made in 1851 and after with the Indians had not worked. The policy of 'concentration' should end. Instead, the Indian tribes should be put separately in small reservations. They would be taught to become farmers and to live the white man's way of life, out of the way of settlers, miners and soldiers.

The two places which they thought to be ideal for this were the Indian Territory of Oklahoma, and the Black Hills of Dakota. The 'Five Civilised Tribes' had been moved to Indian Territory in the 1830s, and these tribes would now be moved to the eastern half, leaving the rest for the tribes of the southern Plains. Nobody thought that any white people would want to settle in the Black Hills. They were far too hilly and a long way from the main routes across the US. This was where the Commission would put the tribes from the northern Plains.

The Medicine Lodge Creek meeting with the southern Plains Indians

The Commissioners first met representatives of the southern Plains tribes at Medicine Lodge Creek in October 1867. The Kiowas and the Comanches had remained peaceful since they had been moved from their old hunting grounds in 1865. They were bribed and threatened until they agreed to take a reservation of 3 million acres between the Red and the Washita Rivers, in Indian Territory. The Cheyennes and the Arapahos accepted a sandy and barren area between the Cimmaron and Arkansas Rivers, also in Indian Territory.

There was to be a separate meeting with the tribes of the northern Plains, in an attempt to end the wars. The Government realised that the main problem was the Bozeman Trail – and by the time the Peace Commissioners reached Fort Laramie in May 1868, it had decided to give way to the Indians and abandon the Trail.

The Fort Laramie Treaty with the northern Plains Indians

On 29 April 1868 the Sioux leader Red Cloud signed a treaty which began:

'From this day forward all war between the parties to this agreement shall forever cease. The government of the United States desires peace, and its honor is hereby pledged to keep it. The Indians desire peace, and they now pledge their honor to maintain it.'

The Government agreed to stop work on the Bozeman Trail, or, as it was called officially, the

Indian reservations in 1875

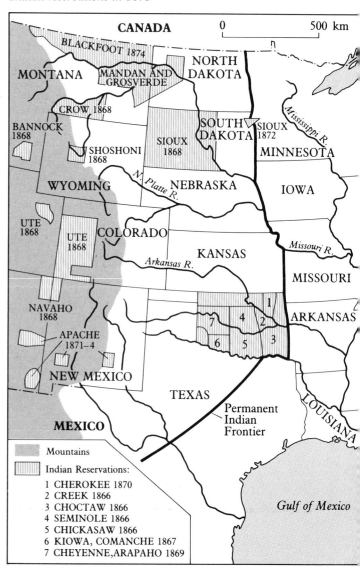

Indian Reservations:
1 CHEROKEE 1870
2 CREEK 1866
3 CHOCTAW 1866
4 SEMINOLE 1866
5 CHICKASAW 1866
6 KIOWA, COMANCHE 1867
7 CHEYENNE, ARAPAHO 1869

Powder River Road. They also promised to abandon the three forts. In return for this, Red Cloud agreed to take his people to a permanent reservation in Dakota, stretching east from the Black Hills to the Missouri. They were to be allowed to use their old hunting grounds in the Big Horn country as long as the Government did not want them.

Red Cloud was pleased with the result of the meeting. When the soldiers had left the forts, he and his warriors burned the forts down. Red Cloud believed that he had won his war.

Small reservations: the answer?

The 'small reservation' policy was also extended to the Rocky Mountain area in the summer and autumn of 1868. The tribes there, like the Ute, the Arapaho, the Shoshoni and the Apache, agreed to go to small reservations scattered throughout Colorado, Idaho, Wyoming, Arizona and New Mexico.

Would Indians and white people both now be able to live as they wished in peace? Each side had problems which made this impossible. The Indians had been put into reservations, but would they stay? The Plains Indians could not live their old, nomadic way of life in these reservations. They usually had to depend on food brought in for them, not hunted. Many of them were miserable, unable to settle to farming, and longed to return to the open plains to hunt buffalo. Many young warriors refused to accept the agreements made by their chiefs, and were prepared to fight for their old way of life. It was difficult for Indians to accept the idea that land could be sold. As Crazy Horse said, 'One does not sell the earth upon which the people walk'.

As far as the white men who signed the treaties were concerned, they were not to know that they would want to use the Black Hills of Dakota in the future. What was more, a treaty could not necessarily change the point of view of those who believed that the Indians should be wiped out. A warning note was sounded by the western military commander when he said in September 1868:

'We have now selected and provided reservations for all off the great road. All who cling to their old hunting grounds are hostile and will remain so till killed off.'

SOURCE WORK: Reservations

SOURCE A

Red Cloud, a Sioux Chief, talks to Colonel Carrington at Ft Laramie in 1866. Soldiers had come to clear the Sioux away from the Bozeman Trail.

'You are the White Eagle who has come to steal the road. The Great Father [the US President] sends us presents and wants us to sell him the road, but the White Chief comes with soldiers to steal it before the Indian says yes or no. I will talk with you no more. I will go now, and I will fight you! As long as I live I will fight you for the last hunting grounds of my people.'
(The US 50th Congress, Senate Executive Document No. 33)

SOURCE B

These are the words of Red Cloud:

'Whose voice was first sounded on this land? The voice of the red people who had bows and arrows. . . . What has been done in my country I did not want, did not ask for it; white people going through my country. . . . When the white man comes in my country he leaves a trail of blood behind him. . . . I have two mountains in that country – the Black Hills and the Big Horn Mountain. I want the Great Father to make no roads through them.'
(Dee Brown, *Bury my Heart at Wounded Knee*)

1 Look back to Chapter 4 and read again what it says about cattlemen and railroads on the Plains. Look also at Chapter 5 and remind yourselves of the way in which the homesteaders began to settle on the Plains.
   a) Use Sources A and B to try to put together the sort of argument which Red Cloud would have used to oppose the building of the Powder River Road (the Bozeman Trail).
   b) What arguments would the Government have used to answer him?

2 Whose fault was it that the policy of 'concentration', and the treaties, like the one made at Fort Laramie in 1851, did not work?

The final conflict: Sheridan, Sherman and Custer

Indians on the war-path

It was not long before trouble began again. The warriors who had refused to accept the Medicine Lodge and Fort Laramie Treaties went on the war-path. Cheyenne, Kiowa, Comanche and Arapaho bands, under Black Kettle, rampaged through Kansas. Soon, other bands were attacking people and destroying property in northern Texas as well.

President Ulysses S. Grant, who took up office in 1869, developed an Indian Peace Policy. He wanted to make sure that the Indian Agents, the white men who were in charge of Indian affairs in the different areas of the West, were the right sort of men. It was important that the Indians should be treated with care and respect. He also tried to see that enough proper supplies reached the Indian reservations. Despite this, the food on some reservations was only fit for pig-swill.

More importantly, the efforts of those who were put in charge of Indian affairs by President Grant could not solve the basic problem. For the whole idea behind the reservations was that Indians should learn the white way of life. They were to learn how to use a plough and reap a crop of corn; to attend school and learn how to read, write and do simple sums.

What Grant and the other humanitarians did not realise was that it was the most difficult thing in the world for Indians to take up the white way of life. In the words of Big Eagle, a Sioux chieftain:

'The whites were always trying to make the Indians give up their life and live like white men – go to farming, work hard and do as they did – and the Indians did not know how to do that, and did not want to anyway.'

If the Indians were to live the white man's life they would have to accept a totally different view of the land, and this was more than many of them could do. If you look back to Chapter 2, page 10, you can read again how Indians thought of their relationship with the land. The white man's view of the land was quite different; he had been told by *his* God 'Be fruitful and multiply, and replenish the earth and subdue it' (Genesis Ch. 1, verse 28 in the Authorised Version of the Bible). What clearer command did man need to till the earth and sow and reap crops?

The Battle of the River Washita

It was the army which really decided the fate of the Indians. Some of the officers disliked the Peace Policy and the reservations as much as some Indians – but for different reasons. The army hardliners wanted the Indians killed off once and for all. General Sherman said in 1868:

General Sherman

General Sheridan

'The more we can kill this year, the less will have to be killed next year. For the more I see of the Indian the more convinced I am that all will have to be killed or maintained as paupers.'

General Philip H. Sheridan, who was in charge of the army in the West, decided to plan a winter campaign. Indians did not, as a rule, roam the Plains in the winter. It would be easier to attack them in their winter camps, for the army could not possibly track down all the roving bands. The plan was to have two columns of troops to drive the Indians into the Washita River Valley in Indian Territory (Oklahoma). Here the main force, commanded by General George A. Custer, would crush the Indians.

Custer had fought in the Civil War, and was a dashing figure who stood out amongst his men, not only for his bravery, but also for his long, flowing, golden hair. Custer was marching with his men from Fort Hays, Kansas, when he came across a fresh Indian trail. Ignoring orders and the planned campaign, he dashed after the Indians until he and his men reached their camp on 26 November 1868. Here was a find indeed! Chief Black Kettle and several hundred Cheyenne and Arapaho warriors had camped for the night. Custer immediately prepared for attack. At dawn Custer and his men rushed on the camp and took the Indians by surprise. After a few hours of hand to hand fighting the Indians were completely defeated. The bodies of 103 Indians, including Black Kettle, lay on the camp ground. Only eleven of these were warriors.

Custer's attack had finally broken the spirits of the Indians in that area. Two months after the Washita River Battle, Custer was able to take the rest of the chiefs to Fort Cobb, on the Washita. There they signed treaties agreeing to go to reservations. The Kiowa and the Comanche were sent to those lands which had been assigned to them in the Medicine Lodge Creek Treaty. The Cheyenne and the Arapaho went to a reservation along the upper Washita River.

The Red River War

Meanwhile, Indian attacks continued in Texas. Major-General William T. Sherman had replaced Sheridan as military commander on the Plains. In 1871 he held a tour of inspection and noticed everywhere signs of Indian attacks and raids. He was in no mood to be kind to the Indians. They must be punished! After a particularly savage Indian attack in 1874, when sixty Texans were killed, Sheridan sent his troops against the Indian bands in the Red River area. War raged throughout the winter, and by the summer of 1875 the Indians could resist no longer. War-weary, half-starved and broken, they went back to their reservations in Indian Territory.

'Attack at dawn'. A painting by C. Schreyvogel of Custer's attack on Black Kettle in his Washita River Valley camp

SOURCE WORK: Attitudes

SOURCE A

An engraving by a white American, showing Indians attacking homesteaders

1 Look carefully at this picture (Source A). How would you use this as evidence of how white people and Indians felt about each other?

SOURCE B

Dee Brown's account of the events after the mustering of the Indians to Fort Cobb, December 1868.

'Yellow Bear of the Arapahos also agreed to bring his people to Fort Cobb. A few days later, Tosawi brought in the first band of Comanches to surrender. When he was presented to Sheridan, Tosawi's eyes brightened. He spoke his own name and added two word of broken English. "Tosawi, good Indian", he said.
   It was then that General Sheridan uttered the immortal words: "The only good Indians I ever saw were dead".'
   (Dee Brown, *Bury my Heart at Wounded Knee*)

SOURCE C

A view from Colonel Ronald S. Mackenzie of the US Army:

'I regard the Cheyenne tribe of Indians, after an acquaintance with quite a number of bands, as the finest body of that race which I have ever met.'
   (Dee Brown, *Bury my Heart at Wounded Knee*)

SOURCE D

'By many the Indian is looked upon as a simple-minded "son of nature", desiring nothing beyond the privilege of roaming and of hunting over the vast unsettled wilds of the West, inheriting and asserting few native rights, and never trespassing on the rights of others. This is equally erroneous with that which regards the Indian as a creature possessing the human form but divested of all other attributes of humanity. Taking him as we find him, we discover in the Indian a subject for thoughtful study and investigation. If I were an Indian, I think that I would greatly prefer to cast my lot among those of my people who adhered to the free open plains, rather than submit to the quiet, unexciting, uneventful life of a reservation.'
   (G. A. Custer, *My Life on the Plains*, Sheldon and Co. 1874)

SOURCE E

'But no-one could be more thoroughly convinced of the treachery and bloodthirsty disposition of the Indians than I am, nor would I ever trust life in their hands except it was to their interest to preserve that life; for no class of beings act so much from self-interest as the Indian.'
   (G. A. Custer, *My Life on the Plains*)

2 Read Sources B–E, and Sherman's words on page 111. Use the evidence from these sources to help you to explain whether or not you agree with these statements:
   a) All army officers were hostile to all Indians.
   b) Some army officers were hostile to some Indians.
   c) People who had a lot of contact with Indians came to respect them.

3 Read the two extracts by Custer (Sources D and E). Both of these are taken from a book which he wrote about his Indian campaigns between 1867 and 1869.
   a) What attitude is he showing towards Indians in each extract?
   b) How could it be possible for one man to hold different views on the same topic?
   c) Would you say, from the evidence in these two sources, that Custer was a 'hard-liner'?

4 a) General Sheridan's words (Source B) and General Sherman's (page 111) have become famous. Why do you think this is?
   b) Look at the photographs of Sherman and Sheridan on page 110. How far can photographs like these help us to understand what sort of men they were?

SOURCE F

Black Elk, Holy Man of the Oglala Sioux:

'It was when I was eleven years old [in 1874] that the first sign of new trouble came to us. Scouts came to us and said that many soldiers had come into the Black Hills. Afterwards I learned that it was Long Hair who had led his soldiers into the Black Hills that summer to see what he could find. He had no right to go there because all that country was ours. Also the Wasichus [white men] had made a treaty with Red Cloud [in 1868] that said it would be ours as long as the grass should grow and water flow. Later I learned that Long Hair had found there much of the yellow metal that makes the Wasichus crazy.'
   (Black Elk in J. Neihardt, *Black Elk Speaks*)

5 Read Black Elk's words in Source F.
   a) Black Elk says that 'Long Hair' had no right to go to the Black Hills 'because all that country was ours'. He goes on to say 'Also the Wasichus had made a treaty with Red Cloud that said it would be ours as

long as the grass should grow and the water flow'.
      Was he right to say that that the Black Hills belonged to the Sioux even before the Fort Laramie Treaty of 1868?
   b) Black Elk seemed to know nothing about the 'yellow metal' apart from the fact that it made white men go crazy. Why not?
   c) If the Sioux did not want the gold, why did they want so much to hold on to the Black Hills?

SOURCE G

Santana, Chief of the Kiowas, speaking in the 1860s:

'I have heard that you intend to settle us on a reservation near the mountains. I don't want to settle. I love to roam over the prairies. There I feel free and happy, but when we settle down we grow pale and die.'
   (Dee Brown, *Bury my Heart at Wounded Knee*)

SOURCE H

Chief Joseph of the Nez Perces:

'The earth was created by the assistance of the sun, and should be left as it was. The earth and myself are of one mind. The measure of the land and the measure of our bodies are the same. . . . I never said the land was mine to do with it as I chose. The one who has the right to dispose of it is the one who has created it. I claim a right to live on my land, and accord you the privilege to live on yours.'
   (Dee Brown, *Bury my Heart at Wounded Knee*)

6 Read what Santana (Source G) and Chief Joseph (Source H) have to say about the Indians' views on life and the land.
   In what ways are these views different from white Americans' views at the same time about the land?

7 How do Sources G and H help to explain the failure of some of the Government's attempts to solve the Indian problem?
   (Clues: you could look at the terms of the Fort Laramie (1851) and Medicine Lodge Creek (1867) Treaties. You could also look at the drawing by Wohaw on page 122).

The Battle of the Little Big Horn: Custer's last stand

Gold in the Black Hills

Just as in the days before the Medicine Lodge Creek and Fort Laramie Treaties, the Sioux were to be the most difficult Indians to subdue. In the early 1870s there was trouble with the Sioux in their Dakota reservation in the Black Hills. They complained that their food was bad and that they had too few blankets. Worse still, the Northern Pacific Railroad was fast approaching their hunting grounds, bringing hordes of hunters who killed buffalo for their skins which they sold in the East. This was another way in which white men and Indians differed. As Chief Satanta of the Kiowa said:

> 'Has the white man become a child that he should recklessly kill and not eat? When the red men slay game, they do so that they may live and not starve.'

General George Custer was put in charge of the soldiers sent to protect the surveyors for the Northern Pacific Railroad against Indian attacks. In 1874 Custer was sent to the Black Hills to find out whether a fort could be built there to protect the railroad. It was then that Custer's men discovered gold in the Black Hills. The Government tried to negotiate with the Sioux to buy back the Black Hills area. Red Cloud demanded $600,000,000. Other Sioux chiefs, however, refused to bargain. The Government failed to get the land, but still decided to open it up to prospectors and miners. Thousands poured in during the winter of 1875, and staked claims to land which the Sioux still saw as theirs by right.

The real trouble began in the winter of 1876. Some Sioux braves were slipping away from the reservations to join Sioux bands like the Hunkpapa, who had not agreed to go to reservations. In December 1875 the Government ordered that all Indians who were not back on their reservations by 31 January, 1876 would be considered to be hostile. This meant that they could be attacked by any troops which came across them. Sitting Bull and Crazy Horse of the Teton Sioux refused to return, and prepared for war. They collected supplies in the Little Big Horn River area. The army was ordered to force them back to their reservation.

The battle which followed between the Sioux and the army ended in one of the worst defeats ever suffered by the US army. Historians have not been able to find out exactly what happened during the battle, mainly because all the soldiers were killed. They have also not really been able to decide why the army suffered such a terrible defeat. You will have to decide these questions for yourself later, when you have seen the evidence. First, read about the events which led up to the Battle of the Little Big Horn. Bear in mind, as you are reading this, anything which could act as a clue to help to explain the unanswered questions about the battle.

The Indians gather at the Rosebud River

During the spring of 1876 thousands of Sioux Indians gathered along the banks of the Rosebud River (see map on page 115). They were angry and worried by the numbers of white men who were swarming over their hunting grounds and killing the buffalo. They were alarmed by the soldiers who patrolled the Black Hills to protect the white men. They felt safer when several tribes were camped together.

The Sioux were joined by bands of Cheyenne and Arapaho Indians. The Sioux, the Cheyennes and the Arapahos all remembered well the times when white men had threatened their people before.

The Sioux Chief, Sitting Bull, had a vision during the sun dance which his tribe held in June 1876. He told the rest of the Indians that he had seen soldiers falling head first into their camp. The Indians believed that this meant that they would defeat the soldiers and so be able to remove the white men from their sacred hunting grounds in the Black Hills.

General George Armstrong Custer

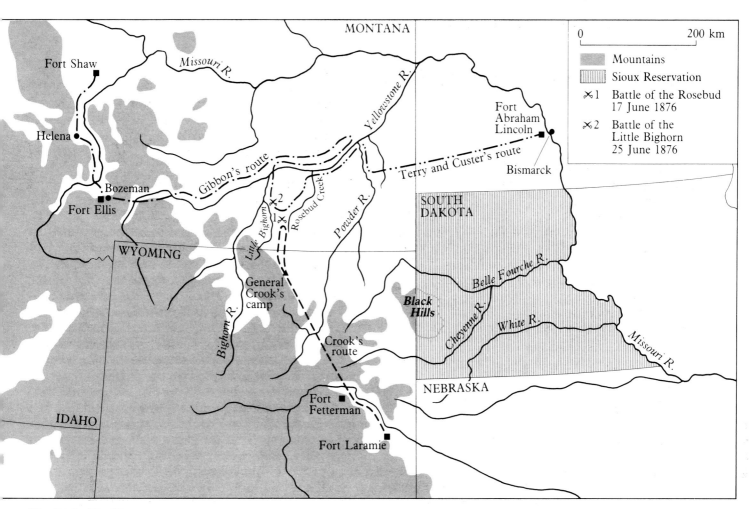

The Little Big Horn area

The army's plan

The army commanders, however, thought differently. Here was a chance to wipe out thousands of hostile Indians! Sheridan ordered Brigadier-General George Crook, who was based at Omaha, to take a column northwards from Fort Fetterman on the upper North Platte; Brigadier-General Alfred H. Terry was to move westwards from Fort Abraham Lincoln; Colonel John Gibbon was to advance eastwards from Fort Ellis in Montana. The man who had been intended to lead this eastward column was General Custer; Custer, however, was in disgrace. He had outraged President Grant by accusing the President's brother of receiving bribes. Custer's command was taken from him. He saw his chance of glory slipping away from him, but thanks to General Terry, he was allowed to go with the eastward column as commander of the 7th US Cavalry.

The first disaster was on 17 June, 1876. General Crook and his column met Chief Crazy Horse with 1000 braves near the source of the Rosebud River. They had been sent south from the main Indian camp to try to stop the advance of the army. Crook was forced to withdraw and the Indians returned to their camp in triumph. At this point, however, the Indian

chiefs decided to move camp west to the valley of the Little Big Horn River. When they had set up camp here there were more than 10,000 squaws, braves and children. Crazy Horse and Sitting Bull had brought their warriors; Red Cloud came with his braves; there were also Arapahos and Cheyennes.

General Terry's and Colonel Gibbons' columns met at the mouth of the Powder River. Terry sent Major Reno to find out where the main Indian force was encamped. Reno discovered the trail left by Crazy Horse's Sioux when they were returning from their defeat of General Crook. This, he found, led westwards towards the Little Big Horn. Terry decided that it was here that they would find the main Indian camp. He sent Colonel Gibbon and his infantry to the mouth of the Little Big Horn to attack from the north. The much faster 7th Cavalry was sent to attack from the south. Terry knew that the cavalry would make a more forceful attack than the infantry, so he offered Custer the help of the companies from the 2nd US Cavalry which had been with Gibbons' force. Custer refused: his men were good enough to take on and defeat any Indians which they may meet. Terry knew very well that Custer was hot-headed and had disobeyed orders before. He therefore gave him his orders in writing, and warned him to keep to these unless there was very good reason for not doing so.

Custer takes matters into his own hands

Custer and the 7th Cavalry set off up the Rosebud River on 24 June. In the evening, after a journey of 46 kilometres, Custer halted his men. Later that evening he heard from his scouts that the Sioux trail had left the Rosebud River and was approaching the Little Big Horn River. Custer made up his mind. He would attack now, without waiting for Colonel Gibbon. Why should any other commander have the glory of defeating the Sioux? His decision not to wait for Colonel Gibbon made a joint attack impossible, and only a joint attack could have trapped the Indians.

Custer knew that his movements had been watched by Sioux scouts and that he could not take the camp by surprise. He would attack at once. He split his men into three divisions. Captain Benteen was sent with 125 men to the south; Major Reno was to advance along the south of a stream which ran into the Little Big Horn. Custer himself would go along the north bank of the stream.

Reno was beaten back after a fierce fight on the banks of the Little Big Horn River. The remnants of his division were met by Benteen and his men as they returned from their southern detour, where they had found no Indians. Benteen immediately realised that Reno needed help. He regrouped Reno's men and did his best to fortify the hilltop which they were occupying. Then they heard gunfire and the sound of battle to the north. That must be Custer! Reno and his men were just setting off to go to Custer's aid when hundreds of Indians appeared and drove them back onto the hilltop. A menacing ring of Indian warriors kept them there until darkness fell.

Meanwhile, Custer was engaged in a fight to the death. On 25 June Chief Gall of the Sioux, who had beaten back Major Reno and his men, charged up from the south. Crazy Horse, who had defeated General Crook, swept right round Custer's position from the north. Other bands surged in, until Custer and his men were surrounded by overwhelming numbers of Indians. Recent archaeological research at the battle site has proved what has been said for many years – that the Indians were impressively armed with the latest repeating rifles. The soldiers used only single-shot Springfield rifles and colt revolvers.

When General Terry arrived on 27 June with the main army, he found the dead bodies of all 225 of Custer's men. Most of them had been stripped, mutilated and scalped. What was strange was that Custer's body was untouched.

A reconstruction of the Battle of the Little Big Horn, painted by Edgar Paxson in 1899 after a good deal of research. You can see Custer in the top centre of the picture

SOURCE WORK: The Battle of the Little Big Horn

SOURCE A

The Battle of the Little Big Horn. A contemporary Indian drawing by Kicking Bear

1 No white man knows for certain what happened during the Battle of the Little Big Horn – and the Indians who survived would not say very much.

Look at Source A. This was drawn by Kicking Bear, and is the only eye-witness painting which is known to exist. Custer is lying to the left of centre, and standing in the centre (left to right) are Sitting Bull, Rain-in-the-Face, Crazy Horse and Kicking Bear. Compare this with the painting by Edgar Paxson opposite.
   a) What differences can you see in the way in which these two artists portray the battle?
   b) What reasons can you suggest for these differences, apart from the fact that one is an eye-witness source and the other is not?
   c) Which of the two do you think is likely to be the more accurate? Why?

SOURCE B

An account of the Battle of the Little Big Horn by an Indian participant:

'There was not much excitement and at first we thought it would be better to surrender as there were so many soldiers in this country, but when Custer came in sight there were not so many, and the word was sent around the camp to get ready. We sneaked from our tents through the tall grass to where our ponies were picketed [*tied up*] and drew them to us by the long ropes. . . . We raced towards the soldiers as the bullets came switching through the grass and through the leaves of the trees.

And we fought, and the soldiers fought, and when we chased the first lot across the river we turned and went for those on the hills. The smoke and dust were very thick – you couldn't see anything and we killed lots of our own men because they got in the way.

Pretty soon the soldiers began to run and we went after them but it wasn't long before they were all killed or wounded. We couldn't tell who was Custer, we couldn't tell anything; their faces were covered with dust and their eyes and mouths were full of it.'
   (B. W. Beacroft, *The Last Fighting Indians of the American West*, Longman 1976)

2 What evidence in this source shows
   a) that the Indians were expecting to find more US soldiers than they did?
   b) that it was difficult to see what happened in the battle because of the dust?

SOURCE C

'Long after the battle, White Bull of the Minneconjous drew four pictographs showing himself grappling with and killing a soldier identified as Custer. Among others who claimed to have killed Custer were Rain-in-the-Face, Flat Hip and Brave Bear. Red Horse said that an unidentified Santee warrior killed Custer. Most Indians who told of the battle said they never saw Custer and did not know who killed him. "We did not know till the fight was over that he was the white chief", Low Dog said.

SOURCE WORK: The Battle of the Little Big Horn (continued)

In an interview given in Canada a year after the battle, Sitting Bull said that he never saw Custer, but that other Indians had seen and recognised him just before he was killed. "He did not wear his long hair as he used to wear it", Sitting Bull said. "It was short, but it was the colour of the grass when the frost comes." But Sitting Bull did not say who killed Custer.

An Arapaho warrior who was riding with the Cheyennes said that Custer was killed by several Indians. "He was dressed in buckskin, coat and pants, and was on his hands and knees, he had been shot through the side, and there was blood coming from his mouth. He seemed to be watching the Indians moving around him. Four soldiers were sitting up around him, but they were all badly wounded All the other soldiers were down. Then the Indians closed in around him, and I did not see any more." '

(Dee Brown, *Bury my Heart at Wounded Knee*)

3 Read Source C.
 a) What similarities and differences can you find in the accounts of Red Horse, Low Dog, Sitting Bull and the unknown Arapaho warrior?
 b) How do Sources B and C back up or contradict the paintings of the battle?
 c) Why do you think so many Indians claimed to have killed Custer?

SOURCE D

Now read this judgement on Custer by a twentieth-century historian.

'Custer was not unsympathetic towards the Indians and their problems, or to their alarm when white settlers encroached on their hunting grounds, and he appreciated their love for a wandering life and the freedom of the Plains. But like others who saw something of their fiendish qualities and unpleasant ways at close quarters, there were certain aspects of the Indian character that he regarded with horror and loathing.

He made many friends among the Indians, who trusted him more than they did most white men; and at the end they showed their regard for him by treating his body with unparalleled respect when it lay on his last field.'

(From the introduction, by Kenneth Fenwick, to Custer's book, *My Life on the Plains*)

4 Is there sufficient evidence in Sources A-D to work out how Custer died? Explain your answer.

SOURCE E

This extract is from an account given by Kate Bighead, a Northern Cheyenne.

'Me-o-tzi [*a Cheyenne woman*] . . . sometimes went riding with General Custer. . . . Later, after he went away, quite a few young Cheyennes wanted to marry her but Me-o-tzi said General Custer was her husband. She told them he had promised to come back to her. . . . Two Southern Cheyenne women were at the Little Bighorn, and when the fighting ended they went to the battlefield. They saw Custer. They knew him well. They had known him in Oklahoma. They recognised him even though his hair was short and his face was dirty. While they stood looking down at him a bunch of Sioux warriors came by and wanted to cut up his body, but these women made signs telling the warriors he was a relative. They did this because of Me-o-tzi. The Sioux cut off one of his fingertips.'

(Evans S. Connell, *Son of the Morning Star*, Pavilion Books 1985)

5 Kenneth Fenwick (Source D), suggests that the reason for Custer not being mutilated and scalped was that the Indians respected his courage. Evans S. Connell (Source E) relates the story that Custer had had a relationship with a Cheyenne woman.

Another suggestion could be that, like many soldiers when they were fighting Indians, he saved the last bullet for himself. Indians did not scalp people who committed suicide.

Which of these suggestions do you think the

more likely? The section in Chapter 2 on the Indians' ideas on bravery, and Source C, might help you explain your answer. Try to work out, also, whether you think that Indians *would* have trusted Custer.

SOURCE F

A twentieth-century view of Custer:

that of general after the end of the Civil War. He finally became a lieutenant-colonel in the Seventh Cavalry, a rank he held until his death. He insisted, however, on being addressed as 'General'. This egocentric psychopath was hard on his men and clearly entertained no humanitarian feelings towards the Indians.'

(G. Schomaekers, *The Wild West*, Macdonald and Jane's 1977)

SOURCE G

Some contemporary views on Custer:

'Some of the officers were friendly and easy-going with their troopers, but Custer struck me as being aloof and removed.'

(Charles A. Windolf, Sergeant, 7th Cavalry)

'I have never met a more enterprising, gallant or dangerous enemy during those four years of terrible war, or a more genial, whole-souled, chivalrous gentleman and friend in peace.'

(T. L. Rosser, former Major General, Confederate Army, speaking of Custer during the Civil War)

'He was too hard on the men and horses. He changed his mind too often. He was always right. He never conferred enough with his officers. When he got a notion, we had to go.'

(Jacob Horner, Corporal, 7th Cavalry)

'The honour of his country weighed lightly in the scale against the "glorious" name of "Geo. A. Custer". The hardships and danger to his men, as well as the probable loss of life were worthy of but little consideration when dim visions of an "eagle" or even a "star" floated before the excited mind of our Lieut. Colonel.'

(Theodore Ewert, Private, 7th Cavalry)

'A man respected and beloved by his followers, who would freely follow him into the "jaws of hell".'

(Mark Kellogg, *New York Herald* correspondent)
(Quotes from D. Nevin, *The Soldiers*, Time Life 1974)

6 Read the different views on Custer in Sources F and G. Notice the following points:
Rosser, a former Major General who fought against Custer during the Civil War, praised Custer; the two men who served under him in the 7th Cavalry did not.
Mark Kellogg from the *New York Herald* praised Custer; most of the soldiers did not.
The secondary source (F) also criticises Custer, but disagrees with Fenwick (Source D) on Custer's attitudes towards Indians.
a) How would you explain the different views?
b) Would you say that Custer was dashing and brave – or ruthless and ambitious? Or could he have been both? Explain your answer by referring as closely as possible to the sources.

SOURCE H

'It had always been General Custer's habit to divide his command when attacking Indian villages. His victory over Black Kettle was obtained in that manner. Had Custer taken his entire regiment into the fight he might still have sustained a repulse, but would have escaped annihilation. It is always a tactical error to divide a small command in face of the enemy. This was Custer's error.'

(J. Finerty, *War Path and Bivouac*, R. R. Donnelly and Sons 1955)

7 Read Sources F, G and H. Look also at pages 114–16 of this chapter.
a) List all the possible reasons for Custer's defeat.
b) Do you think that the 7th Cavalry was defeated at the Battle of the Little Big Horn because there were more Indian warriors than soldiers? Explain your answer.

Was the Battle of the Little Big Horn really a victory for the Indians?

There is no doubt about the fact that the Sioux defeated Custer and the 7th Cavalry in the Battle of the Little Big Horn. It was, however, in the end, no victory for the Indians. In many ways, it hastened their end.

The news of the terrible defeat of General Custer spread quickly. Americans were stunned and horrified. People no longer listened to the humanitarians, and all talk was of crushing the Plains Indians once and for all.

After the battle, the Sioux and the Cheyenne bands went their separate ways, but they were not allowed to get very far. Army divisions, led by General Crook and General Terry, pursued them until they finally gave in. By the autumn of 1876 most had drifted back to their reservations, and in the spring of 1877 even Crazy Horse gave in. Sitting Bull took his people to Canada, where they hoped for British protection. Shortage of food, however, finally forced them to return and surrender in 1881. Crazy Horse had finally been captured and sent to Fort Robinson in September 1877. He was killed, apparently, whilst trying to escape.

The heart had gone out of most of the Sioux and the Cheyenne; all they had was the memory of their great victory at the Little Big Horn. They had lost the Black Hills for good. Was this the end of the Plains Indians? Not quite, as we shall see.

The Ghost Dance

Sitting Bull had not completely given up hope. He was determined to protect and to keep what land his people still had in the Great Sioux Reservation. He would do this not by fighting, but by peaceful discussion. The US Government, on the other hand, were just as determined to take more Sioux land to satisfy the demands of the homesteaders, as well as settlers who were pouring in from Europe.

In October 1890 Kicking Bear, a Minnecongou Indian, came to Sitting Bull with a strange story. A Paiute medicine man, Wokova, had had a vision. This was what his vision told him to say to the Indians:

'All Indians must dance, everywhere, keep on dancing. Pretty soon in next spring Great Spirit come. He bring back all game of every kind. The game be thick everywhere. All dead Indians come back and live again. . . . When Great Spirit comes this way, then all the Indians go to mountains, high up away from whites. Whites can't hurt Indians then. Then while Indians way up high, big flood comes like water and all white people die, get drowned. After that, water go way and then nobody but Indians everywhere and game all kinds thick.'

Sitting Bull was doubtful about this. He did not mind his people learning the Dance of the Ghosts, but he did not want them to be hurt. He feared that soldiers might be sent to stop the dancing. Kicking Bear told him that if they wore special shirts, painted with magic symbols, the soldiers' bullets would not be able to harm them.

The Ghost Dance held a tremendous appeal for the Indians, and soon it was being danced in every Sioux reservation. The Indians became excited. Perhaps they could bring back their dead brothers and sisters; perhaps, soon, the Plains would be covered with herds of buffalo and antelope, as in their old hunting days; perhaps the white man would soon be gone from Indian lands. The Indian Agents began to get seriously worried. Wokova had told the Indians 'You

The Ghost Dance. This photograph of the Arapaho tribe was taken in 1893

must not hurt anybody or do harm to anyone. You must not fight', but some of the dancers held rifles over their heads as they danced, and this worried the white men.

The Ghost Dancers' song

Father, have pity on us
We are crying for thirst
All is gone!
We have nothing to eat
Father, we are poor.
We are very poor.
The buffalo are gone.
They are all gone.
Take pity on us, Father,
We are dancing as you wished
Because you commanded us.
We dance hard,
We dance long –
Have pity,
Father, help us
You are close by in the dark
Hear us and help us.
Take away the white men
Send back the buffalo
We are poor and weak
We can do nothing alone
Help us to be what we once were –
Happy hunters of buffalo.

President Harrison ordered the army to take over control of the Indians. When the army commanders discovered that Sitting Bull was one of the chiefs who was encouraging the Ghost Dance, they immediately sent Reservation Police to arrest him. Many chiefs were involved in the dancing, but Sitting Bull was widely respected and had much influence amongst the Indians. Early on 15 December 1890, forty-three police surrounded Sitting Bull's log cabin. They were soon joined by large numbers of Ghost Dancers, and in the confusion which followed Sitting Bull was shot, together with several other Indians and half a dozen policemen.

The Battle of Wounded Knee

Despite the death of Sitting Bull, the Sioux did not turn to violence. They still wanted to believe that they could bring back their old way of life through their dancing. Big Foot, another Sioux chief, took his people down to Red Cloud's Pine Ridge reservation, thinking that there would be safety in numbers. On the way, they met part of the 7th Cavalry, commanded by Major Whitside. Big Foot was ill with

pneumonia, and was travelling in a wagon. The band surrendered, and all 120 men and 230 women and children were taken to a post at Wounded Knee Creek. They camped there, and were closely guarded in case any tried to escape.

Next morning, the soldiers ordered the Indians to give up their guns and any other weapons. The women and children were told to stand aside whilst they searched the tepees and the men themselves. One young warrior refused to give up his rifle and there was a struggle. A shot was heard, which was later said to have come from his rifle, and the soldiers returned fire. The Indians fought with what weapons they still had, and grappled hand to hand. The soldiers then turned their guns on to the women and the children. Soon Big Foot and most of his people were dead or badly wounded. Many of the wounded crawled away, to die later.

A blizzard prevented the army from removing the bodies of the Indians, and when it stopped, the bodies were found, frozen into strange shapes in the snow. The Indians were buried in a trench, and their Ghost Dance shirts were ripped from them as souvenirs. These shirts had not turned aside the bullets. With Big Foot and his Sioux were buried the last hopes and the last resistance of the Plains Indians.

White Americans called the death of the Sioux at Wounded Knee a battle; they called the death of Custer and the 7th Cavalry at the Little Big Horn a massacre. Do you think that the Indians would have agreed with this?

Big Foot lying dead – and frozen in the snow – on the Wounded Knee battlefield, January 1891

The end of the Indian way of life

The Nez Perce, the Northern Cheyenne and the Apaches

We have followed the story of the Sioux through to its tragic ending. The other tribes fared no better. For example, Chief Joseph and the Nez Perce from the north-western mountains resisted for a while, but in the end had to go to Indian Territory (Oklahoma). Dull Knife, Little Wolf and the Northern Cheyenne also lost heart and were sent to Red Cloud's Pine Ridge Reservation. Geronimo led the Apaches in a fight against the Government from 1881–86, but they too, in the end, surrendered. Chief Joseph probably spoke for them all when he said, on his surrender:

> 'I am tired of fighting. Our chiefs are killed. The old men are all dead . . . . I am tired; my heart is sick and sad. From where the sun now stands I will fight no more forever.'

The Indian problem solved?

With the Indians confined to reservations at last, all their former lands could be opened up fully for homesteaders, railway builders and miners. The Indians had to learn to survive by adopting the white man's way of life.

How did the Indians see their situation? Look at this painting, which was done by Wohaw, a Kiowa. How well he has portrayed the Indians' problem. He turns from the buffalo to face the farm; he rests his foot on ploughed land, as if he is accepting his new way of life.

The Government believed that they had solved the Indian problem. Do you think that they had? Let a white man and a red man have the last words:

> 'I did not know then how much was ended. When I look back now from this high hill of my old age, I can still see the butchered women and children lying heaped and scattered all along the crooked gulch as plain as when I saw them with eyes still young. And I can see that something else died there in the bloody mud, and was buried in the blizzard. A people's dream died there. It was a beautiful dream . . . the nation's hoop is broken and scattered. There is no center any longer, and the sacred tree is dead.'
>
> (Black Elk)

> 'The red man was the true American. They have almost all gone, but will never be forgotten. The history of how they fought for their country is written in blood, a stain that time cannot grind out. Their God was the sun, their church all out doors. Their only book was nature and they knew all the pages.'
>
> (Charles Russell)

Wohaw's painting: 'The Red Man's Dilemma'

SOURCE WORK: Why were the Indians defeated?

SOURCE A

Tall Bull, Southern Cheyenne Dog Soldier Chief, to General W. S. Hancock in 1867.

'We never did the white man any harm; we don't intend to. . . . We are willing to be friends with the white man. . . . The buffalo are diminishing fast. The antelope, that were plenty a few years ago, they are now thin. When they shall all die we shall be hungry; we shall want something to eat, and we will be compelled to come into the fort.'

(Dee Brown, *Bury my Heart at Wounded Knee*)

SOURCE B

This is the view of General Philip Sheridan, US Army:

'These men [*the buffalo hunters*] have done [more] in the last two years, and will do more in the next year, to settle the vexed Indian question, that the entire regular army has done in the last thirty years. . . . Send them powder and lead if you will; but, for the sake of a lasting peace, let them kill, skin and sell until the buffaloes are exterminated.'

(Quoted in J. R. Cook, *The Border and the Buffalo*, Lakeside Press 1938)

SOURCE C

Black Elk remembers:

'That fall [1883], they say, the last of the bison herd was slaughtered by the Wasichus. I can remember when the bison were so many that they could not be counted, but more and more Wasichus came to kill them until there were only heaps of bones scattered where they used to be. The Wasichus did not kill them to eat; they killed them for the metal that makes them crazy, and they took only the hides to sell.'

(Black Elk in J. Neihardt, *Black Elk Speaks*)

SOURCE D

Teddy 'Blue' Abbott, speaking of the professional buffalo hunters:

'When it got dark they would quit, leaving maybe ten or twenty carcasses. Next spring they would just lie there on the prairie and rot, hides and all. It was a waste. All this slaughter was a put up job on the part of the government to control Indians by getting rid of their food supply.'

(E. C. Abbott and H. H. Smith, *We Pointed Them North*, University of Oklahoma Press 1966)

1 Look back to page 16 of Chapter 2 and read Francis Parkman's words about the buffalo and the Indians. Tall Bull's words (Source A), nearly twenty years later, confirm Parkman's fears.
   a) What evidence do Sources B–D give as to why the buffalo were killed?
   b) How true do you think were General Sheridan's words (Source B)?

2 What evidence can you find in the sources to support these statements:
   a) White people had no choice but to slaughter the buffalo.
   b) The Indians could never understand why white men slaughtered buffalo and left their bodies to rot.

3 The Indians may have won the Battle of the Little Big Horn, but they were, in the end, defeated.
   a) Try to work out the *long-term* and *short-term* causes of their defeat.
   b) Which do you think were more important causes than others?
   c) Now try to put together all the reasons for the defeat of the Plains Indians.

8

THE PLAINS ARE CONQUERED: THE CLOSE OF THE FRONTIER

The end of the battle for the Plains

The white man had finally won the battle for the Plains. The Indians had been cleared from their hunting-grounds. There was now nothing to stop white men from claiming and settling the land. They could now put it to the plough, grow crops and use the land as they believed it should be used.

What, though, of the Indians in their reservations? Had the Sioux, brave hunters and conquerors of the 7th US Cavalry, settled down in their reservation on the northern Plains? Would the Cheyenne and the Arapaho, who helped Red Cloud to kill Captain Fetterman and his men, be content to stay in Indian Territory? Mountain Indians like the Ute, the Bannock and the Shoshoni may have found it easier, since they were not nomadic and had never depended on hunting for their food. The Plains Indians, though, with the buffalo gone, could do nothing but accept food sent by the Government. Many were miserable. Many fell ill and died. Geronimo spoke for many Indians, and not just his Apaches on their reservation in Indian Territory, when he said

'Our people are decreasing in numbers here, and will continue to decrease unless they are allowed to return to their native land. There is no climate or soil which is equal to that of Arizona. . . . I want to spend my last days there, and be buried among those mountains. If this could be I might die in peace.'

The end of Indian tribal life

The US Government was also worried, but for different reasons. It believed that until the tribal bonds were broken Indians would not live like white men. It had not been easy for Indians to keep the treaties which the chiefs had signed. The chiefs, as you have seen, had no power to make their people obey the terms of the treaties. If, though, Indians learned to live as individuals who had to obey the law of the land, treaties like this would be unnecessary. A way must be found of ending tribal loyalties. Indians were already being sent to schools to learn to read and write, and to listen to white ways being taught by white people. Now they must learn to live as individuals, not as members of a tribe.

In 1871 Congress had decided that no more treaties should be signed with tribal chiefs. In the early 1880s the Government set up special councils amongst the tribes, to take over the powers which the chiefs had been given by the Government to look after their people. In 1883 special courts took over the chiefs' powers to judge and to punish Indians. In 1885, however, these courts were abolished. In future, the US Federal law courts would keep law and order amongst the Indians on their reservations and punish any wrong-doers. The Indians had lost all their ability to govern themselves.

Land: the white man's solution

Another, more difficult problem was to do with land. The white men and the Indians, as you have seen, had very different views about land and how it should be used. If Indians were to live as white men they must own land individually and farm it. Many white men thought that this was a good idea. The humanitarians believed that the Indians would be better off once they owned their own land. Others encouraged this idea because they realised that if Indians, like the homesteaders, were also given plots of land of a quarter of a section (160 acres), the total area would be far less than that of the reservations. That would then release more land for white settlers.

So when Senator Henry L. Dawes of Massachusetts put forward the General Allotment Act in February 1887, it gained a great deal of support. The Dawes Act enabled the President to grant lands to individual Indians. The reservations, excepting Indian Territory, would be divided up into farms of 160 acres for each adult and 80 acres for each child. The rest of the land on the reservations would be opened up for white settlers.

It all seemed such a good idea, but it would take a lot more than this to make the Indians forget their own way of life. Many Indians would not accept the land. Many of those who did sold it back to white men as soon as they could, for pitifully small amounts of money.

The humanitarians may have thought that they had

solved the problem, but few Indians would have agreed. Unhappy with the land which they had to farm, or landless because they had sold their plot to the first white bidder; without the security of their tribal band and their culture, the Indians became more and more dependent on white people to feed them and give them shelter.

What was not in doubt was that many white Americans were pleased with the 'solution' to the Indian problem. But were the Indians in 'Indian Territory' now safe from land-hungry white people?

The Oklahama land race

On 23 March, 1889 President Harrison announced that 2 million acres in Indian Territory would soon be opened to settlers. This land, the Cherokee Outlet and the Oklahoma District, had been bought from the Creeks and the Seminoles for around $4 million. Settlers had been trying to get this land throughout the 1880s. It was fertile and productive farming land – very attractive to those homesteaders who were still 'busting sods'.

Hundreds of illegal settlers, called 'Boomers', had moved on to Indian lands during the 1880s, but Federal troops had always thrown them out. Railway companies also pressed the Government to open up Indian Territory. Finally, it was to be theirs. The lands would be opened on 22 April. Thousands of hopeful settlers gathered on the edge of the unopened territory a few days before this. At noon on 22 April, bugles, guns and flags told them that they could cross the boundary. Across they rushed, hundreds of them, on horseback or in wagons. By sunset, tent cities stretched along the horizon. By 1905 the Dawes Act was extended to Indian Territory; whites and Indians were to live in a similar way, and Indian Territory was no more. In 1907 Oklahoma was admitted into the Union as a state.

Was this the end of the Plains Indians' way of life? In March 1985 the Supreme Court decided that the Oneida Indians, who had had their lands in the eastern states taken away from them in the late eighteenth century, should be restored to their lands. Is this a pattern for the future? Will the Red Indian ever roam the Prairies again in search of the buffalo? Almost certainly not; the Plains, as we have seen, were not the 'Great American Desert'. The towns and smaller settlements which have grown up on the old hunting grounds will prevent the Plains Indians from returning to their old nomadic ways, however much they want to.

Will other Indian tribes, however, lay claim to their old lands, whether or not they can return to their old way of life? Only time will tell, and *you* must watch out for what happens in the future.

The dash for land in Oklahoma, 22 April 1889

Index

Acknowledgements

We are grateful to the following for permission to reproduce copyright material: Century Hutchinson Ltd and The John Neihardt Trust for extracts from *Black Elk Speaks* by John G. Neihardt. Copyright John G Neihardt Trust (pub. by Simon and Schuster Pocket Books and The University of Nebraska Press); Macmillan Publishing Company for extracts from *Westward Expansion* 4th Edn by Ray Allen Billington. Copyright © 1949, 1960, 1967, 1974 by Macmillan Publishing Company; The State Historical Society of Missouri for a letter by John Marsh; Time-Life Books Inc. for extracts from *The Old West/The Pioneers* by the Editors of Time-Life Books with text by Huston Horn. © 1974 Time-Life Books Inc; TRO Essex Music Ltd/Ludlow Music Inc./Essex Music of Australia Pty Ltd for excerpts from the songs 'The Kansas Line', 'Night Herding Song' (words and music by Harry Stephens), 'Bronc Peeler's Song', all collected, adapted and arranged by John A. Lomax and Alan Lomax. TRO © Copyright 1938, 1966 Ludlow Music Inc. assigned to TRO Essex Music Ltd. International Copyright secured. All rights reserved; University of Oregon Library for a letter by Medorem Crawford.

We are grateful to the following for permission to reproduce photographs: American Museum of Natural History, photo: Arts Council, London, page 10 (centre right); The Architect, The Capitol, Washington, DC, page 22; Archives-American Heritage Center, The University of Wyoming, pages 10 (below), 99 (2); BBC Hulton Picture Library, pages 28 (above), 52; The Bettmann Archive/BBC Hulton Picture Library, pages 32, 43, 125; British Library, pages 58, 76 (above); Denver Public Library, Western History Department, pages 49, 64 (left); Mary Evans Picture Library, pages 7, 53; Thomas Gilcrease Institute of American History and Art, Tulsa, Oklahoma, photo: Courtesy of the Brandywine River Museum, page 94; Courtesy of Glenbow Museum, Calgary, Alberta, page 16; The Granger Collection, page 57 (left); Kansas State Historical Society, page 88; Alfred A. Knopf, Inc: Peter Watts: *A Dictionary of the Old West 1850–1900*, 1977, page 67; Macdonald & Co.: Virginia Luling: *Indians of the North American Plains*, 1978, pages 33 (above), 35 (below); Mansell Collection, pages 13, 19, 68 (below); Missouri Historical Society, page 122; Peter Newark's Western Americana, pages 15, 21, 23, 25, 28 (below), 29, 30, 33 (below), 34, 35 (above), 36, 38, 42, 55, 57 (right) 61, 62, 64 (right) 65, 68 (above), 71, 72, 74, 76 (below), 84, 85, 86, 90, 93, 94 (inset), 98, 110 (2), 111, 112, 114, 116; Courtesy of the New York Historical Society, New York City, pages 44, 73; Northern Natural Gas Company Collection, Joslyn Art Museum, Omaha, Nebraska, page 20; Oklahoma Historical Society, page 12; Oliver & Boyd: Exploring History: Marinell Ash: *Cowboys*, 1984, page 69; *Punch*, page 56; Smithsonian Institution, National Anthropological Archives, Bureau of American Ethnology Collection, pages 120, 121; Solomon D. Butcher Collection, Nebraska State Historical Society, pages 78, 81, 87; Courtesy of Southwest Museum, Los Angeles, California, page 117; Time-Life Books: The Old West/*The Pioneers*, by the Editors of Time-Life Books with text by Huston Horn © 1974 Time-Life Books Inc, page 91 (recipes).
Cover: Detail: 'Across the Continent: Westward the Course of Empire Takes its Way', Currier & Ives, 1868. Photo: Peter Newark's Western Americana.

Source information

Details of source material are given after each extract. If several extracts are taken from the same source, full details appear after the first extract. Where extracts are quoted within the narrative, details are given below:

G. Catlin, *Manners, Customs and Conditions of North American Indian, Vol. 2*, Chatto and Windus 1844, p. 10; G. Grinnell, *When the Buffalo Ran*, Yale University Press 1920, p. 16; F. Parkman, *The Oregon Trail*, Lancer Books 1968, pp. 16, 100; Col. R. I. Dodge, *Hunting Grounds of the Great West*, Chatto and Windus 1877, pp. 20, 58; V. Luling, *Indians of the North American Plains*, Macmillan 1978, p. 32; Chief Luther Standing Bear, *Land of the Spotted Eagle*, Houghton Mifflin 1933, p. 35; J. Chandler, *The Settlement of the American West*, Oxford University Press 1971, pp. 38, 43; B. Currie, *Pioneers in the American West*, Longman 1969, p. 38; J. Applegate, *Recollections of My Boyhood*, Caxton Club Chicago 1934, p. 42; W. Clayton, *A Daily Record of the Journey of the Original Company of the 'Mormon Pioneers'*, 1921, p. 46; R. Billington, *Westward Expansion*, Macmillan 1967, p. 50; H. Greeley, *An Overland Journey from New York to San Francisco, 1859*, Alfred A. Knopf 1964, p. 52; W. P. Webb, *The Great Plains*, University of Nebraska Press 1931, pp. 65, 181; J. and A. Lomax, *Cowboy Songs and Other Frontier Ballads*, Macmillan 1910, pp. 68, 69; R. Santee, *Men and Horses*, The Century Co. 1926, p. 68; E. James, *Early Western Travels Series, Vol. 18*, Arthur H. Clarke Co. 1904–7, p. 74; C. O'Kieffe, *Western Story: the Recollections of C. O'Kieffe*, University of Nebraska Press 1960, pp. 80, 80–1; M. Sanford, *Journal of Mollie D. Sanford 1857–66*, University of Nebraska Press 1959, p. 80; P. M. Angle (ed.), *Narratives of N. H. Letts and T. A. Banning 1925–65*, Lakeside Press 1972, p. 80; C. G. Barns, *The Sod House*, University of Nebraska Press 1970, p. 80; S. Magoffin, *Down the Sante Fe Trail into Mexico*, New Haven 1926, p. 81; Dee Brown, *The Gentle Tamers*, Putnam 1958, p. 81; R. Holt, 'The Pioneer Teacher' in *Sheep and Goat Raiser, Vol. 36*, November 1955, p. 81; G. C. Fite, *The Farmers' Frontier 1865–1900*, University of New Mexico 1966, p. 85; P. J. Broder, *Great Paintings of the American West*, Cross River Press 1979, p. 91; R. May, *The Story of the Wild West*, Hamlyn 1978, p. 99; R. K. Andrist, *The Long Death*, Macmillan 1964, p. 109; Dee Brown, *Bury My Heart at Wounded Knee*, Holt, Rinehart and Winston 1971, pp. 110, 114, 120, 122; B. W. Beacroft and M. A. Smale, *The Making of America*, Longman 1982, p. 121; J. Neihardt, *Black Elk Speaks*, Sphere 1974, p. 122; C. Russell, *Trails Plowed Under*, Doubleday and Co. Inc. 1937, p. 122; S. Barrett, *Geronimo: His Own Story*, Sphere 1974, p. 124.